THE TOYBOY DIARIES

THE TOYBOY DIARIES

Sexploits of an Older Woman

Wendy Salisbury

Old St PUBLISHING

First published in Great Britain 2007 by Old Street Publishing Ltd,
14 Bowling Green Lane, London EC1R 0BD, UK
www.oldstreetpublishing.co.uk

A CIP catalogue record for this book is available from the British
Library.

ISBN13: 978 1 905847 28 0

Printed and bound in Great Britain by CPD Wales
Typeset by Martin Worthington

10 9 8 7 6 5 4 3 2 1

CONTENTS

For the men in my life.
You know who you are...
even if sometimes I didn't.

Names have been changed
throughout to protect the
guilty.

FOREPLAY

This exposé is a sixtieth birthday present to myself, written with my tongue firmly planted in my cheek or, whenever possible, somebody else's. It's an *homage* (or possibly *fromage*) to my past life, a memoir for my future. When I'm slumped drooling in some Senior Sundown comfy chair, someone can read it to me and I can marvel with my last remaining marble that I did *all that*.

Some may find my voice crowing, arrogant and egotistical. They may wish me to fall flat on my face, and in the privacy of my bedroom, I often have. Some may find my adventures hard to swallow, but they are retold exactly as they happened. A woman whose clock is ticking would be a fool not to use her looks, cleavage and well-turned ankle to her full advantage.

When I say I'm sixty, you might get a picture of a little old lady with a tight grey perm queuing up for her pension in the local Post Office. Delete that image immediately!

Think Helen Mirren, Susan Sarandon, Catherine Deneuve, Goldie Hawn, Diane Keaton, Judi Dench, Joanna Lumley – sexy sirens one and all.

I grew up in London in the Swinging Sixties. My father was a physical man who wanted a son but, undeterred by my gender, he taught me to play football, do DIY, read a balance sheet and deal with life like a man. To offset this, my mother sewed relentless little dresses of taffeta and tulle. Confusion reigned and to an extent still does.

At eighteen, I journeyed south to Andalucía to work as an interpreter on the biography of El Cordobés, the world-famous bullfighter. He helped himself to my virginity one hot and sultry Cordovan night – a heady springboard into adulthood.

Twenty years on – two weddings, two divorces and two daughters later – 'Life begins at forty' became my reality and I embraced my single status with a backstage pass that read: Excess All Areas.

My d.o.b. is inescapable, but I laugh in its face and treat it as an aberration on my birth certificate. Like many older people, I still feel like a twenty-year-old. Not every night... but once a week would do nicely. Time is a thief but I've fought it tooth and manicured nail with a dedicated beauty routine and the blessing of good genes from my Russian– Jewish ancestors. My grandmother died at ninety-four, generously legating me her smooth skin and peachy cheekbones. My mother at eighty-six is determined and acerbic still, frustrated even now if a day passes without achievement. The female work ethic rates highly in my family. Aforementioned grandma, widowed at twenty-nine with nothing to eat but two toddlers, taught herself millinery. She became the quintessential matriarch, pushing everyone in her path on to greater accomplishments than her own. When I was fourteen, my Dad got me a job in a restaurant so I could pay for my summer holiday and I have worked almost continuously ever since (though never again as a waitress!). Today, my business is antiques; but although I deal in antiques, I never sleep with them!

My figure is maintained by carb control and yoga, and I'm one of the lucky breed of 21st century *femmes d'un certain âge* who've been there, done that and still look good in the t-shirt.

Like many vital, vibrant women of my generation, I may have another thirty years of love life left. The chances are the best is *not* yet to come and one has to ask oneself: is the pursuit of happiness dependent upon the pursuit of a penis? Is it still possible to flirt, flourish and fornicate into your fifties and beyond? Can you remove your grandchildren's nappies one minute and your lover's Calvins the next? Computer says YES! If, as theorised, men reach their sexual peak at nineteen and women at thirty-five, it follows that at twenty-nine and forty-five they are equally compatible.

So...if fifty-five is the new forty-five...you do the maths.

Not very long ago, you didn't get many firsts after fifty except perhaps fittings for false teeth or a hot flush in the Fuller Figure department. But now, with such variety in society, single sirens are free to celebrate their sexual freedom in whichever way they choose. My personal leaning has always been towards fit young men. Sometimes I've leaned so far, I've actually lost my balance and fallen over. According to current statistics, I'm not alone in my *penchant*. The Noughties man of choice *is* a younger man... the tempting tang of testosterone barely suggested above the lingering scent of mother's milk. And for those playful puppies, the allures of an older woman are manifold: lusty bodies, carnal experience, worldly wisdom, financial security, maternal nurturing and abandoned sensuality.

And a toyboy relationship will never grow old... it's unlikely to last that long.

My age-inappropriate adventures have enriched my life and flattered the very soul of me, even if some of the little buggers failed to turn up when they said they would. Sometimes, in the dark of night, as I lie single in my double bed, I release the catch on my memory bank and tot up my investments. My sex count shows a healthy credit.

My toyboy 'diet' is a recipe for delight or disaster, a Russian roulette of a repast for the sexually carnivorous. But ladies, if you plan to follow my regime, heed this warning:

By all means have your legs in the air, but for God's sake keep your feet on the ground and do not fall in love...for that way madness lies...

RICKY ROTTER

AND THE FOUNTAIN OF YOUTH

Not long after my second divorce, I set off with my sixteen-year-old daughter, Poppy, on a ski trip to the Alps. We flew to Geneva, connected with expedient efficiency to the Swiss railway system and arrived in the village of Villars just as the sun was beginning to set. We checked into our chalet apartment halfway up the slopes, dumped our bags, and stepped out onto the balcony. The *piste* sparkled crispy-white beneath us, like crushed ice spilt from a giant Margarita. Poppy sniffed, shivered and went back inside to unpack. I stayed outside breathing deeply, filling my lungs with cleansing mountain air.

After a few moments, my ears picked up the sound of English voices from the apartment next door. Craning my neck around the frosted-glass divider, I saw two young men lying on their beds and a girl sitting at the dressing-table drying her hair. One of the guys got up, walked over to the terrace door, slid it open and stepped out onto his balcony. I jumped back not wishing to appear 'the nosy neighbour', but he'd spotted me.

'Hi!' he said, looking round from his side of the screen. 'You English? Just got here?'

'Yes,' I replied. 'You?'

'Arrived on Tuesday. You alone?'

'No. I'm with my...' He was extremely fit. Tall, dark, tanned and well-built. What was I going to say? Sister?

'...daughter.' I continued: 'Er...we were wondering where to go for dinner? Anywhere nearby you could recommend?'

'We usually go for a pizza. You're welcome – if you want to join us? I'm Ricky, by the way,' and he reached his hand across to shake mine.

'Hi!' I smiled, wincing slightly at the firmness of his grip, though there's nothing worse than a soggy handshake.

'We'll knock on your door around seven,' he went on, and before I could object, he disappeared back inside.

'I've pulled!' I said to Poppy as I stepped back into the studio room.

'You've *WHAT?*' she demanded, like I'd just told her I'd given her Cabbage Patch Kid to the rag 'n bone man.

'For you, silly!' I explained. 'Gorgeous English guy in the flat next door!'

'M-u-u-um!!' she groaned, throwing her eyes skywards. Then she turned away and continued shoving underwear into the bedside drawer.

At 7.05 p.m., showered and changed into warmer clothing, we opened our door to three fresh faces, made our slightly faltering introductions and crunched down the path to a brightly-lit Italian Bistro. Poppy was quiet and withdrawn at first, but she soon thawed out after a *vin chaud*. The handsome Ricky, whom I thought to be in his mid-twenties, and the girl, Lara, were brother and sister. The other boy, Jason, was their cousin. It was a fun-filled evening full of ski stories, energy and laughter... just what I needed after the traumas of the previous few months.

We all skied together the following day, our new friends leading the way. The first morning in an unfamiliar resort is often daunting: the maps aren't that easy to read, and there's always the danger of ending up on a black run with no way home but down. That night, we dined together again then went on to Le Roc Club in the village. Poppy was now in her element, *tête à tête* with Lara, checking out the local talent.

I left them at the bar and wandered over to the pinball machine. I hadn't played for years and even then only had a vague idea what to do. I put a coin in the slot and the little ball ricocheted forth. Ricky sauntered over and leaned languidly up against the machine.

'Don't embarrass me,' I laughed. 'I'm rubbish.'

Without a word, he stepped behind me, put his arms around my waist and guided my hands with his. Jointly, we flipped the flippers as the little ball pinged frantically to and fro. He stood hard up against me, legs spread, jerking my body from side to side as he concentrated on the game. I could feel his hot breath on the back of my neck and couldn't work out if he was making advances or just showing off his pinball skills with me as the conduit.

Just after midnight, we all left the bar and set off back to the apartment. Ricky fell into step beside me. I looked up at him and raised one eyebrow, but he just smiled enigmatically and kept on walking.

♀

The next day was the last of the old year. I was frankly glad to see the back of it.

'Who fancies the New Year's Eve bash at the hotel tonight?' I suggested as we were finishing lunch. 'And as a thank-you for being such great company, the night's on me!'

Poppy and Lara clasped hands excitedly and started discussing what they were going to wear. Ricky and Jason shared a high five. We decided on an early supper, back to the apartments to get ready and then off to the party.

At 10.30 p.m., dressed in our finest, we crossed the road to join the other revellers at Le Grand Hotel des Neiges. For no apparent reason, Ricky seemed moody. He started drinking quite heavily and mumbled something about hating New Year's Eve. Me too, I agreed as I downed my second kir royale, remembering some truly miserable married ones. The others tried to drag him onto the dance floor but he shook his head and wandered off.

Just before midnight, as the pace was really hotting up, he suddenly re-appeared at my side.

'I'm leaving,' he stated. 'You coming?'

I frowned uncomprehendingly. 'Why?' I protested. 'It's nearly...'

'Precisely!'

And he walked off towards the exit.

I looked around for Poppy and spotted her with Lara cavorting wildly on the dance floor. I turned back and saw Ricky standing impatiently in the doorway staring back at me. The seductive scent of danger inflamed my nostrils, and some corny one-liner popped into my mind: *The only things you regret are those you didn't do.* I felt guilty at leaving my daughter who'd abandoned me anyway, but I really didn't want to spend the chimes of midnight being dragged into a conga line with a load of pissed-up strangers. The ballroom was now a heaving mass of gyrating bodies, flying balloons, deafening music and exploding crackers. I made a rash decision, grabbed my bag and fought my way to Ricky's side.

He grasped my elbow and guided me through the noisy hotel lobby and into the street, walking me briskly back towards the apartments. It was snowing hard. I looked at my watch. It was the dot of midnight.

'Happy New Year to you too!' I said acerbically.

'Yeah...' Ricky muttered and carried on walking.

We hurried in out of the impending blizzard and straight up in the lift to our floor.

'It seems a shame...' I began, but he proceeded resolutely down the corridor. I trotted after him drawn by I knew not what. He stopped outside his apartment, ran his hand along the architrave, found the key, and unlocked the door. He pushed it open and stood aside to let me in. I hesitated for a heartbeat, shot him a quizzical look then moved past him into the untidy room. I felt unnerved, unsure what we were doing here, and mindful that one or all of the others could come back at any moment. The door swung shut and Ricky locked it, took off his leather bomber jacket and slung it over a chair. He turned to face me, reached for my arm and pulled me towards him. I stumbled slightly and fell against him as he grabbed my shoulders to steady me. We looked into each other's eyes for a moment. Then he leaned forward and ran his tongue suggestively along my bottom lip. I melted back against the wall, my knees buckling at the erotic sensation. Ricky took a step forward and pinioned me where I stood. He placed his mouth over mine, and as I opened it to gasp, his hot tongue snaked between my parted lips. Dismay dissolved into desire and I could not help but respond. He pressed up against me, the message obvious through his thick, black jeans.

'What are we doing?' I whispered breathlessly when we came up for air. My insides were curdling with lust.

'What we both want,' he whispered back, a fact of which I had only just become aware.

Alcohol, altitude and the arrogance of youth are a dangerous combination and I succumbed to all three that night. My initial fear of the others coming back was dismissed by the power of a long-unfulfilled sexual craving. Resistance was futile. We undressed hurriedly, reaching out for each other as our excitement mounted. Ricky dragged my panties down and dropped to his knees, plunging his face between my legs, inhaling the woman scent of me. His probing tongue parted my private lips and his moisture mingled with mine. Weakened by longing, I thrust my hips wantonly towards him, submitting to the joy of his lingual lapping. He came up to standing and walked me backwards towards the bed. He tipped me onto it and as I fell, his hands cupped my breasts, his thumbs rubbing the nipples each in turn. Panting now, all efforts at propriety abandoned, my hand shot downwards to grasp the firmness of his long, hard cock. He went down on me again, opening my thighs with a thrust of his head, devouring me with passion and gusto. I bucked urgently against his face and exploded all too quickly as his hungry mouth consumed the flow of pent-up juices pouring forth from me.

Ricky raised himself up and thrust his erection into my welcoming wetness. I cried out at the force of him and hugged my legs around his torso. We ground in rhythm until his body stiffened, froze and then he came, pumping deeply into me as we groaned at the pleasure of his release. He relaxed for a moment, then scooped me up and swung me round on top of him. As my breathing steadied and my hormone rush receded, the full realisation of what we'd just done hit me. The effrontery of it...the gall! He'd played me like a castanet! I propped myself up on one elbow and demanded:

'What on earth made you think...?' then stopped mid-sentence. It was irrelevant now. I'd been a willing participant, but the way he'd assumed I would somehow offended me. My next question shot out unannounced:

'How *old* are you?' I demanded.

'Nineteen,' he replied with no trace of discomfort. My eyes grew wider and I bit down hard on my bottom lip. I didn't know whether to laugh or cry. The last time I looked, I was forty-two.

♀

The next day he completely ignored me. He skied like a demon and sunbathed at lunchtime with his back to me. I couldn't see his eyes through his dark glasses and he kept them on all day. Little shit, I thought, how *dare* you?...and I marvelled at how quickly a woman can get hurt. I hadn't sought this and yet here he was dissing me already! Bastard!

The following day was our last. I was desperate to talk to him but had no idea what to say. My maturity and reason had abandoned me and all I could think to do was play him at his own game, ignoring him even more than he was ignoring me. He'd made me feel vulnerable again, and I'd had enough of that. And I daren't admit I was infatuated. The sex had been electric and I wanted more.

That night we all went out for a farewell fondue. I put on a brave face, but my heart wasn't in it. *No fool like an old fool* kept coming to mind. We were drinking cocktails, Ricky downing two to my one. After dinner Lara and Jason suggested we all go clubbing. I shook my head.

'I've got to pack,' I said, sounding way too mumsy. 'Early start tomorrow...'

'Can I go Mum?' Poppy begged and before I could answer, Ricky looked at me and slurred: 'I'll walk you back.'

I shrugged with indifference but my heart leapt, then landed badly. I wasn't going there again.

We walked in silence, a frosty distance between us. He tripped once and my arm went out automatically to save him.

When we got to the apartments, there was another couple waiting for the lift. We all stepped inside and stood like silent strangers watching the floor numbers light up. Ricky was swaying slightly. I prayed he'd fall and break his fucking neck. Save me the trouble.

I exited the lift ahead of him, strode purposefully to my room, entered, and closed the door firmly behind me. I then leaned against it waiting for a knock which never came.

Anger rose swiftly in me until I was bubbling with fury. Who the hell did he think he was? If he thought he could just pick me up, shag me and dump me, he had another think coming. I paced the floor for a few moments then yanked open the balcony door and stepped outside. The curtains next door were tightly drawn and it was freezing, so I stomped back inside. I tore off my coat and boots then grabbed my suitcase off the floor, hoicked it up onto the bed and started stuffing my clothes in. This did nothing to quell my anger and was totally out of character. I'm a very careful packer. I marched into the bathroom, leaned against the sink and stared at myself in the mirror.

'OK!' I said, as if addressing Ricky. 'You wanna play games? I'll show you games.'

I held my hands under the cold tap and dragged them

dry on a towel. I took a deep breath, then exhaled fully, dropping my shoulders in an effort to calm myself. Then I crossed to the door and eased it quietly open.

I peered left and right along the empty corridor and tiptoed the few steps to the next apartment. I ran my fingers along the architrave until I found the key, unlocked the door as quietly as I could and stepped stealthily inside. The bathroom light was on, casting a single beam across the messy studio room. Ricky was passed out on his bed, his breathing deep and regular. His clothes were in a heap on the floor and the duvet was crumpled up around his waist. I inched forward like a thief, watching him intently for any movement. My heart was pounding, my throat dry. In the half light, he looked like a Renaissance painting: *Adonis Reclining* – a beautiful, young deity, all tousled and muscled. I felt a pang for what we'd shared, but dismissed such tender thoughts as I reached the side of the bed.

With the utmost care, I raised the duvet off him and pulled it aside. He was naked, his meaty penis limp against his well-toned thigh. A whiff of pheromones assailed my nostrils and aroused me despite my cold resolve. Slowly, carefully, I climbed across his legs and straddled him. I held my breath, immobile, but he did not stir. With the gentlest touch, I lifted his flaccid manhood in my right hand, bent my head low and sunk my mouth over it. I teased it lightly with the tip of my tongue, licking and flicking as I cupped his balls softly with the other hand. He sighed and raised his hips, his buttocks clenching as his rapidly rising hard-on swelled to fill my mouth. His eyes were closed, his lips parted, and he began to pant quietly as his head rolled from side to side. Did he think he was dreaming? I bent to the task in hand, sucking rhythmically at first, then harder and faster as I sensed him reaching the point of no return. He was pumping hard into my mouth now, his balls like rocks in the palm of my hand. Just as he was about to climax, I stopped what I was doing and withdrew. His livid prick bobbed frantically about in the air searching for friction, an orifice in which to deliver the goods. I flipped it dismissively with the back of my hand, then climbed off the bed and walked.

'Don't mess with the big girls...' I muttered as I left the room, triumphant in my bitter satisfaction.

Poppy and I flew home early next morning.

I didn't see Ricky again for several years. He went off to university – I went back to my life. Poppy and Lara kept in touch and some time later we all met up again on another ski trip. Ricky had matured considerably and had brought along a pretty, though vacuous, young girlfriend. He seemed slightly embarrassed by her and I picked up the vibe that she irritated him. Occasionally I caught him giving me long, meaningful looks.

One afternoon when I wasn't skiing, having opted instead to sit by the roaring log fire with my feet up reading a book, Ricky returned from the slopes early. As I turned the page, a shadow fell across it and I glanced up to see him standing there, nervously chewing on his bottom lip. It only took one raised eyebrow (mine) and one sideways smile (his) and what happened next was as unpremeditated as it was pleasurable. I can't bear unfinished business, and the afternoon delight under the big Swiss duvet certainly dealt with that.

When time and geography allow, Ricky and I still meet up 'for old times' sake'. We've never really spoken about that first night and I wonder if he may have been too drunk to remember...

Ricky set the benchmark for my toyboy adventures and, although without that heady experience I may have chosen a more conventional route with a lot less aggravation, I would have missed out on some of the best adventures, and sex, of my life...

Ricky: *you ain't no toyboy anymore but thanks for the memory and for providing me with that first intoxicating drink from the fountain of youth...*

MARK ONE AND MARC TWO

THE IN-BETWEENIES

Over the next few years, I concentrated on getting my daughters properly brung up. There was conflict and resolution, laughter and tears, and much hormonal slamming of doors. There were also many comings and goings to and from their respective Dads at weekends and school holidays. Sometimes I had a houseful, sometimes none. I worked hard, embraced my single status, and was always Mummy when required to be.

I built up my career as an antiques dealer, a much-loved hobby which soon became my source of income. Growing up close to Portobello market, it was my joy on a Saturday morning (when I'd finished cleaning my father's shoes for sixpence) to wander around the eclectic stalls fingering the fascinating relics of a bygone age. Years later, one weekend when the girls were off my hands, I was roaming as usual when a beautiful Victorian writing slope caught my eye. It was inlaid with brass and marquetry and although the surface was scratched and the lid was loose, I managed to secure it for £24.00. I was doing an antiques restoration course at the time and this box became my pet project. I eventually sold it for £118.00 and a light bulb went on above my head. With a small bank loan and a big pair of balls, I set up a workshop in Camberwell and was soon employing six cabinet makers restoring antique boxes and furniture which I exported all over the world.

During that time many of my daughters' young friends, both male and female, crossed my threshold. They were like exotic birds with their brightly-coloured clothing and experimental hair. They'd all congregate in the kitchen and I revelled in their company, conversation and music. Crowds of us would decamp with picnics to the old Wembley Station and queue up all day to see Madonna, Michael Jackson, Bruce Springsteen. Then it went all dark and gothic. Black was the new black and, on bad days, the music sounded like 'Songs to Slash your Wrists by'. Later, heavy metal screamed from the speakers, Bon Jovi, Guns 'n Roses, Aerosmith and Testament. I fed off the vibrant energy coursing round my home and some Sunday mornings I'd wake up to a couple of crash helmets on the living-room floor and the sexy smell of grease and leather.

Lara, from the fateful ski trip, came to live in London and some weekends when my daughters were with their Dads, I'd go out with her and her girlfriends. They probably saw me as some kind of Bunny Mother, very different from their own married mums. I was clearly delusional. I saw myself as one of them.

One Saturday night, four of us went to Bar Escoba in South Kensington – three girls in their twenties and forty-something me. We got there early and secured our seats at the bar. As the evening wore on and the place filled up, guys kept jostling us as they reached across to pick up their drinks. This became annoying and we were about to leave when I felt someone tap me on the shoulder. I turned around to see an outstretched hand holding a ten pound note. I followed the hand back up its arm and found myself staring into a pair of the deepest blue eyes with the thickest dark lashes topped by a shock of steel-grey hair. The face was young, smooth and indecently handsome.

'If ah give eeu mah munny, can ya git me a bee-ah?' he asked.

'Sure,' I answered taking the proffered £10 note.

Corona with a slice of lime was the latest fad and I passed it back to him with his change. He wheedled his way through the throng until he was standing by my side. I looked up at him trying to put an age on this striking specimen.

'Cheers!' he said and took a slug and we started chatting. I surreptitiously nudged Lara in the ribs and she pulled a face as if to say: 'How did you do that, you bitch?'

Mark was a hunky 'Sarth Effrican' aged twenty-seven. Like his father and grandfather before him, he had a genetic predisposition to turn grey at an early age. This was very attractive but his face and hair didn't match. Not that I cared. Nothing much matched in my world, apart from my lingerie and shoes and bags. Mark was with a group of work colleagues from the Stock Exchange. They traded futures. My idea of futures was finding someone cute enough to wake up with on a Sunday morning. Mark fitted the bill.

We all joined forces and left Bar Escoba for Shaker, a cocktail lounge on the Old Brompton Road where the city boys started ordering Tequila Slammers and Flaming Ferraris. Two vodka tonics were my limit and I'd had them, but the novelty of watching these guys competing to trash themselves was highly entertaining. Eventually one of them passed out, and, in graceful slo-mo, slithered off his bar stool like a snake, coiling himself in a crumpled heap on the floor. At this point the manager threw us all out.

I found this hilarious. I was forty-six years old and I'd never been thrown out of anywhere before! We rolled the 'body' into the gutter where it proceeded to puke up its week's wages plus bonuses. When he'd finished, Mark heaved him onto his shoulder and carried him home. Lara's friends quit with their morals intact, but she and I were having too much fun, so we followed Mark and his *protégé* back home hooked on the uncertainty of what might happen next.

Mark tipped his workmate onto the bed and left him to sleep it off. He came into the kitchen, where Lara and I stood giggling, and as easy as Sunday morning he began to cut three lines of coke on the granite worktop. Despite growing up in the Swinging Sixties, I'd never taken drugs nor been drawn to do so. I'd had a slice of hash cake and a couple of tokes at a party once and felt like I was flying without wings for a while, but nothing harder than that. I'd always been terrified my head would explode and my tits would drop off. I also hated not being in control.

Confronted with Mark's parallel tracks of Charlie, I felt it my duty to protect young Lara. If I'd been on my own, I may have tried it. After all, you're meant to try everything, aren't you, except incest and country dancing? (Actually I've tried both...but that's another story.) It was now 5 a.m. and we were the last girls standing, but we declined Mark's offer of the rolled-up tenner and watched with morbid fascination as he sniffed the lines. Was he a good bad boy or a bad good boy? I didn't care. He intrigued me and I didn't want it to end there.

Lara was yawning so I said I'd take her home and Mark decided to come with. We dropped her off at her flat in the early dawn and as I approached the corner of my road, the traffic lights turned red. I slowed to a halt and Mark leaned over and planted a juicy wet kiss full on my lips. I adore first kisses. They're like promissory notes or foreign currency: they invoke a sensual journey into uncharted territory. Despite the advent of day, the craziness of the night still lingered and the bitter taste from his tongue fired me up. We carried on kissing as the lights turned green, red then green again. It occurred to me that all the young girls had gone home alone, but I'd pulled a handsome, young buck and it was my moral duty to validate that for the sake of the sisterhood.

As we entered my flat, Mark grabbed hold of me. We made straight for the bedroom where he stripped us both naked and took me standing up on my bed, slamming me into the wall as we bounced to and fro on the springy mattress. I felt strangely wild and abandoned, and reached a screamingly sharp orgasm which I could only put down to the transmission of cocaine. He withdrew at his crucial moment and shot his load all over the flouncy chintz fabric adorning the corona above my bed. Talk about a power shower! We slept most of the next day and I eventually had to throw him out before my girls got home on the Sunday night from their weekend with their Dads.

The following Saturday night, to keep the momentum

going, I decided to throw a party. My youngest daughter, Lily, was at her grandparents for the weekend, but Poppy was at home and she invited some of her friends along. They must have thought it very odd going to her mother's party, but the inducement of free booze and decent grub drew them in. I stipulated to Mark: 'absolutely no drugs' – I had to draw the moral line somewhere. We made jugs of Margaritas and trays of vodka Jello shots and all got very pissed, then someone had the bright idea of putting on the soundtrack to *Grease* which we all performed with raucous, inebriated hilarity. It was one of the best parties I'd ever been to. (I think Lara lost her virginity on my living-room floor that night. She was very quiet and brooding the next day and alluded to it later when the bastard didn't call her.)

I saw Mark intermittently over the next few weekends and we'd spend every Sunday morning at The Hereford pub. The sex was hot but the gloss soon wore off when he started 'borrowing' money from me and not paying me back. Eventually he 'borrowed' a pair of Ray-bans which I never saw again but hey...it was fun while it lasted. It just lasted a little longer than it was fun.

♀

The next romantic interlude was with a very different Marc. He was an ex-boyfriend of Poppy's and we'd always had a soft spot for each other. He'd often arrive way too early to pick Poppy up and we'd have long chats in the kitchen while he was waiting for her to finish getting ready. He had black, spiky hair and beautiful hazel eyes. I'd take a little extra time with my appearance when I knew he was coming round. He was a sweetie, charming and respectful and he brought Poppy a dozen red roses on her 17th birthday. As I arranged them in a vase, he whispered that they were for me to enjoy too.

Around the time she was off to Uni, Marc had family problems and unexpectedly found himself homeless. Poppy suggested in a cavalier fashion that he could move into her room until he got himself sorted. This was like putting a juicy, fat steak just out of reach of a starving carnivore, or frustrated female, in my case...

When Poppy moved out, Marc moved in. Any trauma of her leaving for university (and I did cry for hours the day I dropped her off) was offset by having this manboy under my roof. From day one, there was a tangible chemistry between us. He would leave me little notes and cards everywhere – in the fridge, in the bathroom, on my pillow.

'I love the way you walk.'

'I dreamt of you last night.'

'Shall we get a takeaway later?'

It was totally captivating and I was on permanent heat, dizzy with desire, knowing it was inappropriate, longing for him to make the first move. I had no love interest at the time and invested much emotion and fantasy in the thought of us together. Evenings we were both at home I would cook. He'd bring in treats – smoked salmon, rich dark chocolate, and we'd sit and talk and listen to music, often looking searchingly into each other's eyes. The big ballad heart songs of the eighties were our soundtrack and the electric sexual energy in the air between us could have powered the National Grid. At the end of these passion-fuelled evenings, when I'd long to just drag him off to my bed, we'd always say a chaste goodnight and go off to our separate rooms. It was agonizing and, for once in my life, I had no idea how to play it. Why didn't he try and sleep with me? Was he waiting for me to make the first move? What if I did and he rejected me? Could he not read the longing in my look? One night when he was out with some friends, he phoned me up and told me he loved me. I was sure that night would be the night, but I heard him come in and go straight to bed.

I'd lie awake praying to hear his door open and to feel him slide in beside me...but he never did. We got a little stoned one night and I thought it might happen. We were dancing in the dark and began to kiss but it didn't go any further than that. Maybe I should have just grabbed him...

Eventually Marc sorted himself out and found somewhere else to live. He still came to visit occasionally and he remained the object of my fantasies for a very long time. Much later I discovered through some throwaway remark of my daughter's that he was rather under-endowed in the dick department. Maybe that was why he'd never consummated our mental affair. He would have hated me knowing that...not that it would have mattered. I utterly adored him, and I have no doubt he felt the same.

♀

After Marc, I dated a lot of men my own age and had an eighteen-month relationship with one of them, but no one really rocked my world until I met Tom...

23

TOM

THE SEVEN-YEAR GLITCH

(...AND I ONLY EXPECTED SEVEN MINUTES...)

Once my youngest daughter, Lily, had left for university, I decided to put my flat on the market. I needed a change of scene and a new project to keep me busy. I was not in a particularly good place and there's not a mother alive, whether married or single, who is ever really ready for the empty nest.

On the day she left, I veered between a stiff upper lip and quivering lower one. Lily's best friend Fiona was also going to Bristol, and her mother offered to drive us up in her 4 x 4. Fiona's sister and the dog came too. On the drive west, the girls chattered excitedly about their futures, whilst I sat huddled in the back watching the autumn landscape whizzing past the window. It was a drizzly afternoon in late September. The old gold trees leaned into autumn like ageing spinsters – drying, dying...The windscreen wipers swished back and forth like a monotonous metronome: *you'll be all alone...you'll be all alone...*they seemed to say. Depression draped itself around me like a worn grey mantle and I sank down in the seat feeling wretched and forlorn. Once or twice Lily gave me a 'you'll-be-OK-Mum' look and squeezed my hand, which only made matters worse.

Once we arrived at the university campus, we helped the girls to unload their cases, carrier bags and boxes into the Hall of Residence. It was a slightly run-down, ivy-clad Georgian manor house which in any other circumstances would have been charming. But the thought of my little girl living there with no Flash-fresh bathroom, home-cooked meals or Mummy-in-the-night filled me with dismay. The girls' bedroom was cold, grimy and basic, haunted by the spirits of long-departed students whose blood, sweat, tears, vomit and fag ash were undoubtedly ingrained into the threadbare excuse for a rug which covered the old oak floorboards. Under the worn and wonky mantel stood one of those lethal gas fires, the sort that leaks deadly fumes all through the night, and they all wake up dead. I shuddered, and the taste of bile rose to my throat. I fussed around trying to make it homey but it was a thankless task, and eventually it was time to leave.

'Right!' said Fiona's mother officiously, slamming the book on my daughter's childhood. As far as she was concerned, everything was tickety-boo. She then thumped Fiona on the back and barked:

'Goodbye old chap! See you at Christmas!' and marched off down the corridor without a backward glance.

Lily and I stood facing each other, aware that the moment of parting had finally come. She fell around my neck and we clung to each other sobbing like war-torn refugees. We're Jewish. It's in our genes. We've been oppressed. Some of our ancestors put their six-year-olds on trains out of Germany and never saw them again. I hugged and kissed her desperately, then tore myself away mumbling: 'Speak later...' and blurred off down the stairs and back to the car.

Fiona's mother was busy re-arranging empty boxes in the boot. I gave her a watery smile but there was cold comfort there. The little sister had commandeered the front seat with the dog, so I returned to my corner in the back and continued my journey of self-pity all the way home. They banged on about hounds and horses oblivious to my pathetic sniffling. I didn't give a fuck about the sorry state of Bandit's front fetlock. All I could think about was that this so-called 'first day of the rest of my life' felt like the 'last day of the best of my life'.

'You don't know how lucky you are,' my friends with younger children had said when I told them Lily was off to Uni. 'All that space and freedom, no faddy meals to cook, full power over the remote control, no teenage hormones to deal with, no blaring music...' But that was what I had thrived on. Well maybe not *all* the music...

♀

I'd made advance arrangements for the next fourteen nights, terminally afraid of being Home Alone. I began a drama course, went to see plays and films, cooked dinner for friends, re-arranged my knicker drawer, re-painted the kitchen, spent hours on the phone to everyone I knew and some I didn't, and generally did everything to avoid life on my own. Industry cures melancholy, or so they say.

A few weeks later, feeling more together and with the flat in tip-top order, I phoned the local estate agent and arranged an appointment for 3 p.m. the following afternoon.

♀

The street door buzzed and I let him in. I could hear footsteps coming up the common stairs and I opened the door to not one but two tall, young men both booted and suited. Adrian, the stocky one, entered first and shook my hand as his eyes scanned the entrance hall. On his heels came a keen, young chap with a floppy hairdo holding a clipboard. His tie was over his shoulder like he'd been running for a bus. The minute he saw me he whipped off his glasses and a light beamed out of his eyes and lit me up. He introduced himself as Tom.

I showed them around, and they measured up. We agreed on an asking price and I said I'd pop into the office next day to go through the details. Tom shook my hand warmly as they left and said there were applicants on his books he was sure would like it. He called me early next morning to arrange a viewing. I wanted to stay in Maida Vale so he was also going to try and find me something else.

Over the course of the next few weeks, I saw Tom six or seven times. Every time we met, our conversations became a little more personal: what we'd done over the weekend, books we were reading, films we'd enjoyed, some family stuff. One sunny October afternoon he took me to view a ground-floor flat with a gorgeous garden. The owners were away. There were two deckchairs on the lawn so we sat down and relaxed, even helping ourselves to a couple of beers from the fridge. This felt very naughty and he later replaced them! Tom clearly had no urge to get back to the office and I was more than happy to spend extra time with him. I really enjoyed his company – he had a great sense of humour and boundless energy. Plus I'd developed a bit of a crush on him and his attention to me was very flattering. When he told me he was going away that weekend to try and patch things up with his girlfriend, I felt an irrational pang of jealousy. A girlfriend? How dare he! For some stupid reason, this really pissed me off.

One evening, about two months after we'd first met, he brought an applicant round to see my flat. Immediately after they left, my doorbell rang again. I thought he'd probably forgotten something so I buzzed him back in and he bounded up the stairs then stood in the hallway shuffling his feet.

'She really likes it...' he said running his fingers nervously through his hair. 'I think she'll put in an offer.'

Good, I thought, but you could have told me that over the phone. He appeared to have something else on his mind but no words were forthcoming.

'Have you got any more appointments tonight?' I asked filling the gap.

'No,' he replied. 'I've finished for the day, thank God...'

'Would you like a coffee?' I offered and like a puppy, his tail started wagging.

We sat down at the kitchen table and Tom chattered incessantly for half an hour – I have no idea about what. I was watching him, liking what I saw, wishing I had a man like him, sorry I wasn't wearing more frivolous earrings. Also, for once, I wasn't getting ready to go out. Eventually, he ran out of steam and looked at his watch.

'Better go...' he said, somewhat apologetically, and we both stood up.

I walked him to the door, and again he hesitated, shuffling his feet. I looked up at him and raised my eyebrows enquiringly.

'Are you...?'

'I...er...there's something I've been meaning to tell you...'

We both spoke at once.

'Yes...?' I encouraged, opening my eyes wider.

'Ireallyfancyyou'.

He blurted it out in one long stream then dropped his head, unable to look at me.

'Oh!' I laughed out loud with pleasure and relief, my spirits soaring with surprise. 'I really fancy you too! And I'm *so* glad *you* said it, because I *never* would have.'

We sort of fell towards each other then and I thought he was going to kiss me, but we banged heads then noses, and hugged awkwardly as I tried not to get make-up on his suit.

'Do you want to stay for something to eat?' I suggested, aware that this *diem* needed *carpe*-ing.

'I can't,' he answered regretfully. 'I'm meeting friends at 8.30.'

'Oh...' I said again, unable to hide my disappointment.

What's the point in declaring yourself, matey, if you're not going to do anything about it?

'I could cut it short and come round later?' he ventured. 'About 10? 10.30, if that's not too late?'

I perked up and nodded eagerly.

'Fine!' I said. 'Call me. I'll be here. I'm not going anywhere.'

And he kissed me briefly on the lips and hared off down the stairs as if to make later arrive sooner.

I closed the door behind him and did that thing where you lean against it and slide down slowly onto the floor. I was all of a dither, giddy with excitement and brimming with anticipation. What a result! I then did a quick body check and realised pretty much everything needed doing.

I dashed into the kitchen, crashed the cups into the sink and went straight to the bathroom to run a bath. I undressed hurriedly and ran my hand up and down my left leg. It felt like a gooseberry. I always had my legs waxed but hadn't been recently. My bikini line was rambling, my toenail varnish chipped and my armpits were fuzzy. In the absence of a man, personal maintenance had become somewhat relaxed. I conjured up a mental image of a picture palace organist playing *The Flight of the Bumblebee* as I began a speeded-up version of 'A Day at the Beauty Parlour'. I showered, body-brushed, exfoliated, shaved, plucked, primped, scrubbed, buffed, polished and moisturised until I was shiny as a new pin. Bleeding in places, but shiny. I washed and dried my hair, slathered myself with Clinique Aromatics Elixir body lotion and ripped out the entire contents of my wardrobe, eventually settling on pale pink lingerie, pale blue jeans and a white shirt with the top three buttons undone. I then poured myself a large Scotch and ginger, cracked in some ice and waited for the phone to ring...and waited and waited and waited.

I was starving by this time, but didn't want to eat anything lest it swell up my stomach. I eventually relented and peeled a carrot, then ate a slice of cheddar then went back to the bathroom to re-brush my teeth for fear of smelling cheesy. Eventually, after much angst and pacing, the bloody phone finally rang. Anxiety relaxed into relief.

'Hi!' he said. 'I'm just leaving Wandsworth. Be about half an hour?'

Renewed vitality coursed through my veins. He was on his way! I topped up my drink and continued pacing, pausing occasionally to fluff up my hair in the mirror. At last, at 10.35 p.m., the doorbell rang. I buzzed him in and he took the stairs two at a time and delivered himself smiling to my door.

Tom was wearing jeans and a check shirt and it occurred to me that I'd only ever seen him in a suit. He looked much younger in casual clothes. This was not necessarily a good thing given the already considerable age gap, but frankly my dear...who gave a damn?

He was carrying two bottles of wine, one red and one white.

'I bought one of each...' he explained placing them on the kitchen counter, '...not sure what you like.'

I stepped forward and put my arms around his neck.

'I like *you,*' I said brazenly, the Scotch talking. He hugged me tightly and lowered his forehead to rest against mine. Tom was 5'11½" and I was barefoot, which made me seem petite and vulnerable. Men like this. It brings out the best in them.

He opened the red wine and we went upstairs to my loft-style living-room and settled ourselves on the sofa. I was fully expecting him to jump on me, but he didn't, which was both refreshing and frustrating. He was obviously a slow man. I was trying not to be a fast woman.

Tom began to nuzzle me gently around my ears and neck, inhaling my skin and smelling my hair. I breathed him in deeply and we were like two feral creatures testing the taste and scent of each other. I stretched languidly back onto the couch and tugged him towards me, and so began a long, slow seduction, each embrace and caress filling me with longing and desire. We paused occasionally to sip our wine, passing little drizzles back and forth into each other's mouths. At one point, Tom missed and the wine trickled down my neck. I tensed as I thought it might stain my cream silk sofa, but giggled instead as he caught it with his tongue which he ran from my clavicle back up to my lips. I raised myself up and turned off the lights. I lit a candle, changed the CD and returned to the couch. Lying side by side, I threw my leg across him, tilting my pelvis forward in a clear invitation. Tom rolled on top of me and a provocative moan escaped from deep in my throat. We were still both fully clothed but my hand went down his back and slid inside his jeans where I was surprised to encounter a pair of bare buttocks.

'You haven't got any pants on!' I chided, in a voice reserved for telling off the children.

'No...' he answered affirmatively. 'Sometimes I don't.'

This conjured up all sorts of images of the appointments we'd been on with him, unbeknown to me, swinging commando inside his business suit.

We continued our gentle exploration of each other. I let Tom dictate the pace. I longed to lure him to the bedroom, but he seemed content just kissing and caressing. I relaxed against him, melting like cold butter on a hot crumpet, floating in a blissful balance of high arousal and low resistance. Eventually in the early hours of the morning, I managed to entice him into my bed.

'We'll be more comfortable,' I whispered insistingly. 'We don't have to *do* anything...I just want to feel you...hold you...against me...'

Just saying this made me quicken. I'd been hovering on the edge of paradise for so long and I prayed he would weaken once we were flesh to flesh. But when we got into bed, he still did not take me as I craved him to do.

'What's the hurry?' he whispered, stroking my face. 'Let's save it...' and of course he was right. And this *not* making love was so much more potent than making it.

His behaviour, however, did confuse me. If he'd fancied me for so long, and here I was offering myself to him, if not on a plate then on a pair of very expensive Descamps sheets, then why was he resisting me? I wasn't used to this kind of treatment – or respect – if that's what it was. Whether or not he knew it, he was being very clever: in this case, less was definitely more.

Tom and I lay fused together as close as two separate beings could be *sans pénétration*. His erection dominated the space between us and I wriggled down towards it but he pulled me back up. Strange boy, I thought. What was he afraid of? And what exquisite torment was this? I was practically sobbing for a climax, and yet I did not want this sweet agony to end. My viscera pulsed with every heartbeat, my yearning for him more palpable with every touch. If falling in love was something tangible, then I held it in my hands that night; the strength of emotion between us was a living, breathing thing.

My curtains were wide open and a silent moon observed us – beaming down as we took time out from our suppressed passion to doze on and off in each other's arms. I would have happily died that night, or made a pact with the devil for the moment to last forever. I prayed that for once in eternity the sun would forget to rise...that the world would stay dark and demon daybreak would never come.

At 3.48 a.m. our euphoria was shattered by the strident and persistent buzzing of the street door bell. Tom leapt out of bed, snatched his jeans off the floor, hopped clumsily into them and dashed to the entry phone. He grabbed it off the wall and shouted 'Stop that now! I'm coming down!'

I shot up to sitting, the sheet gathered round me, my dream state shattered by this rudest awakening. I glared uncomprehendingly at him as he struggled to button his shirt.

'*Who the hell...?!*' I spat, all tenderness dissipated.

'I'm sorry, I'm sorry...' he stuttered as he tore barefoot out the front door, slamming it as he galloped down the stairs.

Dazed and confused, I got out of bed, shrugged on my robe and reeled out of the bedroom. Who the fuck had rung my doorbell in the middle of the night and how come he'd known who it was?! The girlfriend presumably! So he was just another adulterous bastard after all!? But how *could* he be? We hadn't even done anything. Or maybe *that* was why...But he'd been so sweet, so loving...we'd been in Heaven, now it was all shot to Hell.

I could hear raised voices on the common staircase. I wondered if I dared open my front door, firstly to shush them – afraid of what the neighbours might think – and secondly to see what this bitch looked like. I had no intention, however, of putting myself in the firing line of some volatile nutcase who might pound up the stairs and stab me in the neck. I could hear her shouting: 'Who is she? Who is she?' and him answering: 'No one. It's nothing. Anyway, I've told you – it's over.'

Thanks, I thought cynically, so now I'm 'no one, nothing'. And what was 'over'? Her or me?

I got dressed. It made me feel less vulnerable, as I stood with my ear pressed up against my front door. I could hear their voices rising and falling but I couldn't make out the words. He was stressing some point quite intently, and she was crying, and then sobbing inarticulately. Eventually, I heard them both descend the stairs and exit the building. Tom's brown suede safari boots were still in my entrance hall. I looked out of the bedroom window and saw him leading an unsteady, reluctant blonde across the road to a double-parked car with its hazard lights flashing. He manhandled her into it, bent down to say something, then he slammed the driver's door and she crashed the gears and drove off.

He walked slowly back across the road, his fists clenched

angrily at his sides. He stopped at his own car and put his hands on the roof then started banging his head hard against it, a systematic, self-destructive pendulum of punishment. I stood at my window and watched him, trying to process my own feelings. He returned to my building and tapped the doorbell for a millisecond. I buzzed him in. He dragged himself slowly up the stairs, entered my front door and fell to his knees before me. He hugged his arms around my legs burying his face in my thighs.

'I'm sorry...I'm so sorry...' he repeated, his voice quite desolate and distressed.

'Just go!' I said angrily, unwilling to deal with this at 4.30 in the morning. 'How dare you bring your problems to my door? And how the hell did she know where you were?'

'She's a nutter,' he answered. 'I can't get rid of her. She's already been unfaithful twice and I've told her it's over a million times... She's been ringing all the bells in the road! She saw my car...'

I pulled away from him and huffed off into the kitchen. He flopped down dejectedly and pulled his boots on. I picked up his keys from the worktop where he'd dropped them a lifetime ago and threw them at him. He left them where they landed, stood up and made to approach me but I put my hand out to stop him.

'GO!' I ordered, feeling more disillusioned than I could ever remember.

Tom gave me a lingering look, scooped up his keys and slunk off miserably down the stairs.

I was too wired and incensed to cry. I lit a cigarette (I hadn't smoked in ages) then stubbed it out because it tasted foul. I brushed my teeth, creamed off the remains of my make-up, got undressed and went back to bed.

♀

I must have fallen asleep eventually as the next thing I knew it was morning and the phone was ringing.

'Can I come and see you?' asked Tom in the humblest voice.

'Well you certainly owe me an explanation,' I retorted, as the night's events came flooding back.

'One o'clock,' I commanded. 'I'll give you fifteen minutes.' And I slammed the phone down.

I fought a variety of emotions that morning. Self-reproach at having been made a fool of, slighted that he hadn't wanted to make love to me, and shame at having reached the so-called 'age of experience' without being able to judge a good character from a bad one. At one o'clock, my mouth set in a don't-bullshit-me line, I opened my door to the most enormous arrangement of flowers I had ever seen in my life. The beribboned bouquet had legs encased in charcoal grey trousers and was wearing Chelsea boots. I ushered it into the kitchen where it was lowered onto the table. Behind it stood a very sheepish Tom. Unsmiling, I remained on guard with my arms folded and an *it-better-be-good* look upon my face.

The story was a longer version of what he'd told me the night before. He assured me he'd spoken to her that morning, that it was definitely over, that he never wanted to see her again, that he'd told her he was in love with someone else. (Really?! *Moi*?) He asked what he could do to make amends. He had dark circles under his eyes, his hands were shaking and he was clearly a nervous wreck. I was now cool, calm and collected. Back in the Mother Ship's self-control room, normal service had been resumed.

'Well I *could* give you one more chance...' I granted, after a seemingly long deliberation, reprieving the convicted infidel on his way to the gallows. I remembered the feel of his thick, hard cock against my thigh. I wasn't going to let that get away without a fight.

'But if you ever...'

He stopped me in mid-stream, shaking his head violently.

'I won't. I promise. Let me cook you dinner Saturday night. I'd love to do that for you.'

And so it came to pass that the following Saturday evening Tom entered my home and my life with two carrier bags from Waitrose and a video of *From Here to Eternity*. He laboured long and hard over the stuffed courgettes which were delicious, but we never made it to dessert and we never watched the video. And he never went home again... until nearly seven years later...when the relationship ended and he moved out.

Introducing him to my daughters was something I was proud to do but also put off for as long as possible. They knew I often had some nefarious goings-on about which they really Did Not Want To Know. No children want to contemplate their parents' sex lives even if the parents are married to each other. But once Tom was ensconced under my roof it became inevitable that he should meet the 'fokkers'. I tried to find a common bond between them which, apart from their ages – which were a lot closer to his than mine – turned out to be football. He was a keen Chelsea fan and my girls had followed their Dads and were Spurs supporters. Poppy came round to meet him one Saturday afternoon, and I was glad to hear them chatting about goal averages and league tables as I played Mum preparing tea in the kitchen. She told me later she really liked him but was a) afraid I'd make a fool of myself and b) worried that I'd get hurt. In a mother/daughter role reversal, I understood she was only trying to protect me. She was also over one Saturday evening when he got five numbers up on the lottery. I could hear them both screaming at the TV and ran in to find them jumping up and down hugging each other. (He only won a measly £1,100 which was very disappointing!)

The rest of my family were, if not a little bemused, accepting and circumspect; they were, I suppose, happy to see me happy, and my mother always welcomed us to her table for our Jewish Friday night dinners. Tom was such a charming, funny, easy-going, generous-spirited guy you couldn't help but like him. I'm sure my ex-husbands had plenty to say behind my back, but I never heard it and I didn't want to. They met him on the odd family occasion and were, to their credit, respectful and friendly. It was nobody's business but mine anyway, and I knew the condemners and critics amongst my peers were only jealous. I've always lived my life my way and no amount of disapproval is ever going to change that!

When Lily was back from Uni for the holidays we all lived together in peaceful harmony. Once she'd got used to Tom, he became like a big brother to her and she kept in touch with him for a while after we split up. It was a loss for all of us...

I used to get a bit miffed when I heard them giggling together the minute I left the room, and I went back in one time and asked what the big joke was all about. It transpired they'd both been holding farts in but had relaxed as soon as I was out of earshot. It also used to infuriate me when I got all dolled up to go to the theatre on a Saturday night and Tom would emerge in jeans and trainers. I'm anal about certain things and worried that we wouldn't match, but Tom wasn't. Tom was always just himself.

I'd asked him early on about wanting his own children, but he professed not to be bothered. I told him he could stay with me and share my grandchildren which he happily agreed to do. My baby granddaughter adored him. She was three when he left and I know she missed him terribly. She would look at me with big sad eyes and ask 'When's Tom coming back to play?' and the lump in my throat would swell up like an injury. I found her once gazing at a photo of him with tears coursing down her little cheeks and I swear I felt my heart break.

I was forty-nine when we'd met; he was twenty-seven. We spent my fiftieth birthday skiing in Aspen and his thirtieth travelling in Argentina. Once or twice during our years together he dropped to his knees and begged: 'Marry me', but I'd laugh him off in a very cavalier fashion. We'd exchanged rings and our own vows one Sunday morning in bed, and that was as married as I wanted to be. I loved him but I recognised the imbalances between us. He filled my body, but he never quite managed to fill my mind.

Much of the time we led a quiet, contented, home-based life. Most nights we'd have our dinner in front of the TV and then play Scrabble. Sometimes he'd call me from work at 6 p.m. and ask if I wanted to go out for a pizza but I always refused as I'd planned the evening meal long before then and expected him home at 7 p.m. I realised afterwards that I stilted his spontaneity and I should have accepted his invitations and thrown the duck breasts in the bin. Maybe we'd have communicated better face to face in a restaurant instead of side by side watching EastEnders...

Conversation was never very high on Tom's agenda and eventually I missed the mental buzz of adult repartee. This didn't alter the fact that when we split up it broke my heart and my world fell apart. I hadn't reckoned on him taking my soul with him when he left. I missed the relationship terribly and I felt fragile and frightened to be alone again at fifty-six. I cried every day for the first year and it was a long and laborious effort of self-love and determination to rebuild the me I used to be.

And I still can't listen to Dinah Washington singing Mad About the Boy without a wistful sigh of nostalgia for those – the calmest, quietest, most peaceful years of my life...

ALONE AGAIN

FROM THE PITZ TO THE RITZ

The full realisation of 'the end of the affair' really hit me when I finally found the courage to go home to my flat on the day Tom moved out. For weeks beforehand, we both had our own mental struggle accepting it was over, and had spent many nights clinging together crying, whilst totally unable to vocalise our feelings. Tom was never very communicative at the best of times, and in the lead-up to our parting he had become deeply depressed, morbidly inarticulate and darkly moody. When I asked him what was wrong, he'd just shrug and mumble 'Don't know' like a confused child. We went to a relationship counsellor once at his suggestion, but I arrogantly fobbed off any need to go again from my point of view, so we let it drop.

I'd gone out with a girlfriend the night before he left, as watching him pack would have been impossible for me. When I got home after a tearful dinner, I turned towards the bedroom, although he was sitting in the kitchen. The door to the study was closed which was unusual. I opened it tentatively and peered inside. A mess of overstuffed black sacks filled the room. Seeing his belongings piled up like those of a refugee made my stomach lurch, and my heart sank with a stultifying sadness. With a trembling hand, I took a sheet of A4 paper from my printer and wailed **WHY?** across it in huge black print. I placed it on top of the pile and closed the study door. Dread and fear flooded through me as I crept into bed for our last night together. Even when Tom finally joined me some time after 2 a.m. we lay apart and did not speak.

Our relationship had been no toyboy fling. Despite the twenty-year age gap, we'd been a committed couple, and perhaps because of our differences, had both made the extra effort to make it work. And it had worked until the time when it worked no longer. Like a device which needed batteries, our connection slowed down, faltered once or twice and then stopped. This break-up was, in many ways, harder than ending my marriages, which had failed for fundamental and tangible reasons. With Tom it was nebulous. We'd always got on, had never argued or become embittered or bogged down with money problems and monotony. The truth was it had run its course and I was getting bored.

Around that time, by a quirk of accidental timing, Oliver, a business colleague turned personal friend of mine, hit a brick wall in his marriage. He had recently discovered his very posh wife *in flagrante* with a local labourer and had fallen apart, throwing himself headlong into a complete mental breakdown. My life being on an even keel (or so I thought) I took his problems on as a project, making myself available at all hours of the day and night as his shoulder to cry on and personal confidante. From his rehab clinic in the depths of the Kent countryside, he underwent some kind of emotional transference and imagined himself in love with me. This was very flattering and after nearly seven years with the same man, I guess I had a little itch. Oliver texted, phoned and wrote to me constantly and because I had nothing better to do, I responded the same way. We planned to escape our humdrum lives and build a future together in the luscious surroundings of the Hotel du Cap Eden-Roc, where we would drink champagne and eat caviar on the terrace at sundown for the rest of our lives. I'm not sure who was the madder, him or me...

My involvement with Oliver led to my neglect of Tom who was suffering his own hour of need to which I was oblivious. The final nail in the coffin was hammered in one Sunday morning, while Tom was slumped on the sofa watching the motor racing. I was in a confrontational mood and I put Carole King on my bedroom stereo and turned the volume up to blaring during the chorus of *It's Too Late:*

> *It's too late baby, now it's too late,*
> *Though we really did try to make it*
> *Something inside has died*
> *and I can't hide and I just can't fake it...*

to which I sung along at the top of my voice trying to provoke a reaction.

The next evening, I went into the bathroom while Tom was in the bath and he was reading a piece of paper. I assumed it to be Chelsea's football fixtures for the coming season so I ignored it, but I found the paper later on screwed up in my waste bin. It was the entire lyrics of *It's Too Late*, which he'd downloaded off the internet and had been studying. The message could not have been clearer, but instead of sitting down with him to discuss this, I ignored it. He must have thought me a complete cow but, in my defence, whenever I tried to broach the subject of 'us', I'd get a blank look and no response.

So while I was busy offering me and sympathy to someone else instead of putting my own house in order, Tom quietly decided it was time to move on. For the seven years we'd been together, from boyhood to manhood, he'd been totally integrated into my lifestyle and my family and I don't think he knew who he was any more. In California-speak, he needed to go off and find himself.

The lead-up to his departure was interrupted by 9/11 which, for a couple of weeks, gave us something to talk about. But the inevitable day finally dawned and with much trepidation, I returned home after work that evening to a hauntingly empty flat. As I stepped across the threshold, the door got stuck on something and I saw that he'd put his keys back through the letter box. This seemed brutally final, and a stabbing pain hit me full in the chest. There were huge gaps on my shelves where his books, CDs and general stuff had been and one wardrobe door was gaping open, the hangers dangling empty and lifeless from the brass rail. There were also several open and empty drawers. As Carole King said: 'Something inside has died'...

I reeled with disbelief that he had actually gone and began a fit of trembling as I sank down sobbing onto the bedroom floor. I'd never really expected him to leave. It was Tom and I, me and Tom. We were a couple. He was my partner, my lover, my manchild, my trophy boy. And now he was no more and I was alone again at FIFTY-SIX! With the children gone and no one to focus on but myself, panic set in, my emotions in turmoil. My brain began whirring like the engine room of *Titanic* just after the iceberg debacle.

How on earth was I going to survive? What in Heaven's name would I do?

♀

When you've lived with someone for so long, the first few weeks after the break-up are strange times indeed. You have two options: you can either sit huddled in a corner, a bottle of gin in one hand, a fag in the other, howling the lyrics to all those love songs or...you can get up, get dressed and get out. I chose Option Two. I went out. Every night. Every single night, so incapable was I of staying home and facing my solitude. I went to the cinema, the theatre, pubs, clubs, wine bars, restaurants, galleries, cultural talks, city walks – the opening of a tin of tuna if I thought there'd be people there. Even the gym held a certain appeal, for verily it is written: misery loves company. When I did find myself home alone, I had the TV and radio blaring and was on the phone non-stop. Bewitched, bothered and bewildered was I.

Although I had undoubtedly instigated the break-up, the minute Tom exited my life, he rose like a phoenix from the ashes of our relationship onto the world's highest pedestal, re-born in my imagination as The King of Rock 'n Roll. This is called 'idealising' – where you forget all the crap that went before and replace it with a rose-tinted perception of how wonderful that person was, how idyllic your time together had been, and the perfect juxtaposition you and he occupied in each other's lives. And in truth, I'd really appreciated the years we'd shared. It may sound trivial but out at the cinema on a Saturday night, if I saw a group of women together, I'd hold his hand a little tighter and thank God I wasn't one of them. Because despite being the autonomous person I have since become, I still believe that having a man on your arm gives you validation and status...and it was ever thus.

To help myself through the traumatic early weeks, I tried a myriad of ways to make myself go off Tom. I made a list of all the things that had really irritated me about him: the fact that he loved all sports, bought and wore the wrong shoes, constantly flipped channels, expelled noxious gasses, repeated the same jokes, and was incapable of picking up glaringly obvious hints on birthdays and Christmas, as well as his socks from the bedroom floor. During that highly emotional time, listening to any kind of music was completely off limits. Every word was a personal message; every melancholic note killing me softly with its song. Thank God I discovered Radio Four.

In my quest to recapture the me I used to be, I turned to alternative therapies. I would have tried anything to stop the crying; no matter how many deep breaths I took, a daily stream of salty tears ran roughshod down my cheeks, with scant respect for my make-up. In order to heal and rebalance my missing mind, I found myself, one cloudy, grey afternoon, entering the hallowed portals of Thirty-Three Belgrave Square, 'The Spiritual Society of Great Britain'. This organisation, manned by lank-haired vegetarians in Friends of the Earth shoes and hand-knitted tank tops, occupies a building in the poshest part of London, conservatively worth around £20m. It's an upstairs, downstairs sort of house, all Adam fireplaces, soaring ceilings, elaborate mouldings and cornices, panelled walls and a sweeping mahogany staircase that begs descent in a taffeta ball gown. I approached the bespectacled geek at the front desk with nervous trepidation.

'Spiritual healing?' I enquired quietly, my voice embarrassed to admit out loud that I needed it.

'Turn left, down the stairs, along the corridor, first door

on the right.'

'What? *Now?*' I croaked, unprepared for the immediacy of his response. I had wanted to pick up a leaflet, study it, book an appointment, come back later maybe, think about it for a year or two.

'First-come first-served,' he smiled and gestured over there.

I descended a narrow flight to the mansion's basement. The floor was covered in pre-war linoleum with a genuine craquelure finish; the walls were glazed in a dusty shade of greige. As I crept along the dimly-lit passageway, I could hear whale music playing. I entered a large, sparse room divided laterally by a series of hospital screens. On one screen was pinned a typed notice:

'Silence please. Healing in progress.'

On the left stood a rickety old table with a pile of flyers and a donation box. I was uncertain what to do next, but a runner seemed like a good idea. As I was pondering this option, something moved in the corner of my eye and there slowly appeared from behind one of the screens the shiny, bald pate and wide, staring eyes of a tall, black gentleman. As he emerged into full view, I noted the large wooden crucifix around his neck and the fact that he looked exactly like TV chef Ainsley Harriott. Could this be a wind-up?

The healer walked slowly towards me and without a word, he took my coat. He motioned me towards a metal-framed chair where I sat down rather stiffly.

'It's my first time,' I whispered, a spiritual virgin up for sacrifice.

'My hands may get hot, my hands may get cold,' he intoned deeply in the voice Paul Robeson used to sing *Old Man River*. The music warbled on, reminiscent of Chilled Ibiza and mystic meditation. And then he laid his hands on me. I breathed deeply and tried to relax.

I thought about what had brought me to this place, to sit before a stranger who was pressing his palms firmly into my back. Once or twice I nearly lost it, hysteria mounting inside me and threatening to explode in an outbreak of sobs or hyenic laughter. But I did not succumb to these temptations. Instead I continued to take long, slow, deep breaths, forcing myself to go with the flow and benefit in whichever way possible from this strange experience. The mood was broken somewhat when the tape stopped with a loud retro clunk and he had to turn it over, but his hands did get hot and they did get cold. After fifteen minutes or so, he stepped away from me and bowed. I thanked him, returned upstairs and paid at the desk with my credit card. Nice to know that the spirits accept plastic.

When I left, I did feel calmer – and clearer – but I never went again. I continued my self-help regime with yoga and Pilates, drew some energy from the power of crystals, burned incense and bathed nightly by candlelight with lavender oil and patchouli.

I went a bit New Age and after about a year, my heart began to mend.

Oliver, the catalyst behind the break-up between Tom and me, limped on with his loveless marriage. He did like to talk about it and these conversations usually took place across the crisp white tablecloths of London's finest eateries, often ending up on the dance floor at Annabel's. Who was I to complain? Although our 'love affair' had come to nothing, I'm a sucker for a good night out, and we're still great friends.

Despite an attempt to date once or twice after we broke up, I never heard from Tom again. He's married now and I truly hope he's happy.

JAKE

Whole in One

During the testing After-Tom time, while I was still sailing the bad ship *Cry-a-lot* and trying to stay afloat through the depths and shallows of being single again at a very uncertain age, I noticed an advert for a Kabbalah Lecture one Sunday afternoon at Regent's College. (This was way before Madonna forced Kabbalah onto the front pages, but not in a good way.) I'd never been particularly interested in sects or alternative religions, but not wishing to experience yet another Suicide Sunday I opted to continue my search for spiritual enlightenment and a deeper insight into the meaning of life. (Could it simply be chocolate?)

There is always an ulterior motive to these sorties of mine. You never know who you might meet and I must have had some kind of premonition that day because after I parked my car in the Outer Circle of Regent's Park, I tidied the messy heap of Sunday papers strewn in the foot well into a neat pile. Why I imagined someone might be getting into my car after the lecture, God only knew...

True to my worst expectations, the gathering comprised 80 per cent women and 20 per cent men, most of whom were opinionated pontificators bent on talking rather than listening. For the uninitiated, 'The Wisdom of Kabbalah' claims to be 'an instruction manual for life' – a way of tapping into a realm that lies beyond our five senses and into the source of intuition, i.e. our sixth sense, believed to be the origin of pleasure, joy, healing and happiness. 'Discover How to Play the Game of Life and Win' goes the blurb. Yeah, right, pass the Bendicks Mints.

Trying to keep an open mind and optimistic bent at all times, I listened intently as the over-enthusiastic saleswoman, sorry – lecturer – assured us that miracles *can* happen, total fulfilment *is* possible, the mystery of the universe *shall* be solved, and peace and harmony *could* be ours once we'd whipped out our cheque books and signed up for the eight-week course. Shoving my cynicism aside – luckily there were two empty chairs beside me – I scanned the assembled throng to gauge the general reaction. As I glanced left and right, my eyes suddenly lit on the face of an angel, sitting to my right at the end of my row. He was a young man incandescent with perfect beatitude. I imagined I had already been transported to a higher plane and it hadn't cost me a penny! How could I not have noticed him earlier? How come my G.B.A. (Gorgeous Bloke Alert) hadn't gone off? As I gawped in admiration at this dark-haired, blue-eyed, tan-skinned demi-god, he stared right back at me in a manner unbefitting such an ethereal creature. His look was so intimate, so carnal, I felt like I'd been licked. And then he smiled. And the sun came out. And all the loss and loneliness of the past six months just melted away... His smile plugged my broken heart back into its socket and the current zig-zagged through it strong and true. I knew I was alive again.

The rest of the lecture passed in a blur. Every time I glanced at him, he was looking unashamedly back at me. I became self-conscious of my every move; my body language screamed Woman Interested in Nearby Man, as I crossed and uncrossed my legs, ran my fingers through my hair, cupped my face in my palm, folded my arms then unfolded them again, stuck out my chest and lifted my chin. All this was a (not so vain) attempt to appear younger, taller and prettier in order to ensnare The Beautiful Boy.

When the lecture ended, the audience mingled out into the hallway. I had no further business there, but I firmly believe that fate sometimes needs a helping hand. Like God said to the man praying to win the lottery: 'Morrie! Meet me halfway...at least buy a ticket!' I'd bought my ticket and I intended to get my money's worth.

As I exited the lecture hall I spotted The B.B. talking with some other young people. I hovered nearby pretending to study the flyers on the notice board, picked up and quickly dropped the £5.00 Kaballah bracelets (strings of red thread to ward off the evil eye!) and £4.00 bottles of Pure Kaballah Water (gulp!) I generally wasted as much time as possible until there were few enough people left for him to notice me again. As he started saying goodbye to his friends, I went out onto the landing, positioning myself where he inevitably had to pass, and so as to appear to have a life, I made a mock mobile phone call, talking into the handset in an animated fashion. As he walked past me, I said brightly 'OK. See you later then. Bye' and fell into step alongside him down the stairs. He looked around and smiled that smile again and asked me what I'd thought about the lecture. We continued chatting as we walked together across the courtyard and out into the spring sunshine of Regent's Park.

'Where are you off to now?' I asked coquettishly, hoping beyond hope the answer would be 'nowhere.'

'I'm going over to some friends in South London,' he replied.

My heart sank.

'You wouldn't know where the nearest tube station is, would you?' he continued. 'I'm Jake, by the way.'

'Wendy,' and I smiled my sweetest smile as we shook hands and said Hi.

'Baker Street is just round the corner,' I told him, certain that he must know that. 'I could give you a lift?'

Einstein said: 'Imagination is more important than knowledge.' My imagination was running wild and I couldn't bear to let this opportunity pass.

And so the handsome, young stranger climbed into my tidy car.

The Power of Kabbalah? Possibly, although both of us later agreed we had no intention of doing the course.

♀

I took the most circuitous route possible the few hundred yards to Baker Street Station. I would have gone via Venus if I'd had enough petrol. He told me he'd just finished with his girlfriend of five years and at twenty-nine how strange it was being single again.

'Tell me about it!' I replied, affirming my similar single status (though not my age!).

'I've just finished with my boyfriend of nearly seven years,' I said wistfully. 'It's a tough period of re-adjustment, isn't it?'

And then, all too soon, we arrived at the station. I stopped the car, switched off the engine and turned to look at him. He looked straight back at me. I was lost in sin and it must have shown in my eyes.

'Gimme your number!' he requested abruptly and my heart sang as I dictated it. He entered it straight into his mobile phone, then pecked me on both cheeks, said: 'See ya!' and leapt from the car, weaving in and out of the oncoming traffic before disappearing down into the depths of the underground.

I was riveted to the spot, mouth gaping, mesmerised and hypnotised. Like some exquisite dragonfly, he'd settled on me for an instant, allowed me to admire him, then spread his wings and flown away.

I stayed parked in my car for a long while, shaking my head in wonderment at how such a fleeting meeting had altered my mindset and re-affirmed all possibilities. There *would* be love after Tom. I just had to be in the right place at the right time. And even if I never saw Jake again, he'd re-awakened my sense of self and restored to me something I thought I'd lost forever: my essential Wendiness.

On the way home, I pondered the effects that people have as they enter and exit our lives. They stamp their footprints on our brains, in our hearts and sometimes on our souls. If all goes well, they will enrich us and bring out our best qualities, like Michelangelo releasing the sculptures from their marble confines. If it goes badly, they will diminish us, eroding our spirits, wasting our resources, draining our energies, leaving us dry and unfulfilled. Physically people can probably live without each other. Mentally and emotionally, it's another matter.

What do we want from life? The stock answers are: peace of mind, love, health, fulfilment, harmony and good fortune. But what we really need to enjoy a tranquil existence is self-sufficiency, which is *our* destiny as determined by *our* actions, not those of others. At the risk of coming over all Self-Help Manual, we cannot rely on other people for our happiness; it is not their responsibility.

It may be a soppy song lyric, but learning to love yourself *is* the greatest love of all and the hardest to achieve. We look in the mirror and do not see the big picture. We see that we are too short and too heavy, and we focus on our bad hair, dry skin, big bum, small tits and bemoan these physical facts without looking within to see what really counts. Then the criticism would really begin, for who wants to admit to being guilty of any of the Deadly Sins, let alone all seven? (I got stuck halfway through trying to remember all these, then had to go out to meet a friend for dinner. Right next door to the restaurant was a bar which listed its cocktails on a menu in the window: Pride, Envy, Wrath, Sloth, Avarice, Gluttony and Lust. I thought it and it appeared before me. How random was that?)

The person who arrived home from the Kabbalah lecture was very different from the one who'd set out earlier that day. And imagine my absolute delight when later that same afternoon, Jake texted me.

Gr8 meeting you. Lets do it again to which I replied Love to. Where and when?

Annoyingly, he failed to reply and I had a terrible job restraining myself from texting him again.

♀

I thought about Jake a lot over the next few days but decided not to take any action. Maybe what we'd had was all there'd be, and I'd all but given up when I got another text from him:

Sorry. Been busy. Fancy meeting up for a drink?

Well you could have prised me off the ceiling with a crowbar! Ignoring the rules of texting I fired one straight back and we made an arrangement for him to come over for dinner the very next evening. The thrill of this chase had a finite conclusion and there was no point in beating about the bush. As far as I was concerned, the timing was perfect. The next day was Tom's birthday – the first one since we'd been apart. And I'd heard somewhere that the best way to get over one man is to get under another.

I thrust through the next day like a bitch on heat and picked Jake up at Maida Vale Station at 7 p.m. I'd prepared a light summer supper of Parma ham and melon, smoked chicken, avocado and roast pepper salad, and fresh berries and cream to be washed down with a nice, cold bottle of my favourite rosé, Domaine d'Ott. As I drove up to the station however, the heavens opened and I couldn't see out through the windscreen for the torrents of rain lashing against the pane. I was peering left and right trying to spot him when the car door was wrenched open and a very wet and dripping Jake dived in, steaming up the interior as he shook water all over me. His hair was soaked, his clothes sodden and droplets were coursing all down his face. He resembled an adorable little puppy who'd fallen in a pond and I just looked at him and burst out laughing. If he'd been hoping for the suave sophisticated approach, he'd been scuppered. I ran the back of my hand slowly up his wet cheek and my eyes softened in adoration at the very fact of him. He flashed me his winning smile and leaned over and kissed me on the mouth. With no further ado, I floored the accelerator and we sped home.

Once indoors, I let Jake use the bathroom to dry off while I opened the wine, although he'd been thoughtful enough to bring a bottle with him. I managed to resist suggesting he take all his clothes off immediately...though the thought of it made my cheeks flush and my heart flutter.

Conversation was no problem. He was very chatty and relaxed and made himself at home in my kitchen while I finished preparing the supper. As I was slicing the avocado, he came up behind me and put his arms around me, then lifted my hair and kissed me lightly on the back of my neck. I quivered from my nose to my toes and I swallowed hard to still my rapid breathing.

After dinner, we went into the living-room and I put some music on. (This is often a problem area with a younger man as tastes do vary, but now that Robbie and Rod have recorded the classics, I can get away with it. Yeah!)

Jake told me about his plans to go to L.A. and work on a film script and I listened with interest, murmuring words of praise and encouragement. While he spoke I marvelled at the serendipity of life, and I thanked the God of Chance Meetings for bringing us together. I got up to change the CD and when I turned Jake was standing behind me. He grabbed hold of me and kissed me hungrily, a moist and penetrating kiss, the effects of which spread through me like molten lava. Not taking my mouth off his, I eased him backwards along the corridor, our fervour growing with every step. We just made it through the bedroom door as he lowered me down onto the floor and began to divest me of my clothing. When I was down to my lacy lingerie (and poised provocatively beneath him) he stood spread-legged above me and took off his own clothes. I looked up admiringly. I was seeing things from a very different angle, and I began to crawl my way up his naked leg towards the firm, young flesh standing to attention above me. This had the effect of tripping his love switch and he turned into a Olympian sex god going for gold.

Back to front and inside out he took me, delighting and exciting every inch of me, provoking my wildest delirium time and time again. Jake delivered the entire Kama Sutra in one sitting (lying, kneeling, standing, twisting, turning) and I blessed the fact that I was yoga fit and bendy. My joy and ecstasy rang out around my room and blew away the ghosts who'd heard me sobbing through so many lonely nights.

We finished our fuck fest flat out on the floor – sweating, panting, gasping and laughing. It was the most life-enhancing, liberating and fulfilling sex I had ever had. I was fifty-six. He was twenty-nine.

Once we were able to move, we staggered up to standing and tottered off to shower; then we climbed exhausted into bed, where we slept wrapped and raptured in each other's arms. I had no idea he was going to stay the night. This was indeed a bonus. He snored like a train but I didn't care. I didn't want to sleep anyway. I just wanted to lie there with my brain smiling and my body tingling, rewinding the wonders of man and woman.

In the early hours, when he spooned into me with a renewed hard-on, I slid down the bed and pleasured him again. He grunted with satisfaction and mumbled: 'Than' you ver' much' and I let him go back to sleep. I felt totally happy, my head, heart, blood, organs, bones and viscera reborn and renewed.

At around 7.30 a.m. Jake got up and padded off to the shower room. I opened one eye to watch him go. I admire a pair of fine, firm buttocks even if they are walking away from me. I turned over and threw my arm across my eyes to deny the inevitable advent of day. As I heard Jake turn on the shower, I went into my ensuite and sat down gingerly on the bidet allowing the jet of warm water to soothe my sore and tender private parts. Ah! The agonising ecstasy of internal bruising: the pleasure pain that brings a secret smile to your face every time you remember how you got it. I brushed my teeth, cleaned off the smudged remains of last night's make-up, re-applied some mascara and a little foundation, slipped into a lilac satin nightie and popped back into bed just before Jake emerged from the guest bathroom wearing The Robe.

The Robe deserves its own mention. It had been purchased several years before, at great expense, from Gucci in Bond Street. It was fashioned in that densely-woven towelling you only find in the very best hotels with a pile so thick you can hardly shut your suitcase when you try to nick one. Of course, they're wise to this now and charge it to your credit card. The Robe had a shawl collar edged in navy and a chic GG logo embroidered in red and gold on the breast pocket. I had bought it way back when for the love of my life, the Master of my Universe, seven years into my second marriage, which had seriously started to itch. I'd met him on a business trip and we'd fallen madly in lust, travelling the world to be together whenever possible. I used to take The Robe with me, though he hardly ever wore it as we spent most of our time writhing naked on a succession of king-sized beds in the Leading Hotels of the World.

When we inevitably split up, I kept custody of The Robe and had laid it to rest in my ottoman until my big sort-out after Tom had left. I couldn't bear to get rid of it so I hung it behind the bathroom door where it remained: limp, flaccid, unloved and unworn until that morning, years of tears later, when Jake emerged fresh and fluffy from his shower.

He walked over to the bed, presumed me to still be asleep and trotted off to put the kettle on. I listened to the kitchen noises and when I heard the click of china on my bedside table and smelt the rising aroma of freshly-brewed coffee, I opened my eyes. Jake was standing over me, clad in The Robe like it was his due. I propped myself up on one elbow and effected a gentle stretch and yawn, using the time to process a distortion of mixed feelings.

The Robe was, to my mind, a sacred vestment, rather like the Turin Shroud but by a better designer. It reminded me of whose it was, why I'd bought it, when he'd worn it, where it landed when he took it off and why it had been unworn since the day we parted. Seeing another man wearing it was both a desecration of my lover's memory and a rebirth for what was, essentially, a fairly useless piece of kit. I decided to embrace the fact that it now graced another man's back and determined that from that day forth it would be donned by as many lovers as possible, worn open for ease of groping, and closed for the pleasure of undoing its belt and delighting in the contents within.

I drank my coffee, then got up and made us scrambled eggs on toast for breakfast. And then Jake had to go. I was starting to come down from my high, feeling strained and weepy through lack of sleep. A need and yearning clutched my heart, and I knew I could not ask the inevitable question: when will I see you again? You have to face the fact that these true-life fantasies are fleeting and when they're over, you're in danger of feeling more alone than you did before. If you adopt the right philosophy, i.e. 'tis better to have loved and lost...you realise that any notches on the bedpost, even if they damage the woodwork, are better than no notches at all. And I wouldn't have missed this particular notch for the world.

Jake left as he'd arrived, with a smile on his face and a kiss on my lips. I fought the urge to disappear back under the duvet and forced myself to stay up and do some yoga. Then I had a long, hot shower and told myself that I'd been gifted with what many women, no matter their age, would give their last dime for: a night of passion with a hot, young stud. Jake texted me an effusive thank-you later that day which made me clutch my mobile tenderly to my breast and rock it like a baby.

The May Bank Holiday was looming so I texted him a few days later and asked if he fancied coming to The Little Venice Carnival – subtext: *I'd really like to fuck you again.* He said he'd let me know, which was par for the course, as these guys rarely make arrangements in advance. Eventually we settled on the Sunday afternoon, which threw me into a state of ecstatic euphoria as I planned hours of unrivalled hedonism and endless delight. I decided to push the boat out and bought a whole fridge full of gourmandises from the hugely expensive local deli: a jar of Beluga caviar, some pâté de foie gras, wild smoked salmon, white truffle and porcini pasta, Nepalese pine nuts from the foothills of the Himalayas and a tub of Black Swan and Tamarind ice cream. I was clearly thinking (and spending) with my 'dick'.

I was not prepared for the fact that the little shit who'd shown me Paradise just two weeks before was about to diss me in the most soul-destroying way by simply not turning up. While I waited for him, my mood plummeted from the heights of heaven to the depths of hell. I gave him half an hour which I extended every half an hour until he was over two hours late. I kept trying his mobile but it was switched off and despite leaving several messages which began with an upbeat: 'Hey baby! Where a-r-e you?' and ended with a menacing: 'You'd-better-be-fucking-dead-in-the-gutter-cause-that's-the-only-excuse-I'll-accept!!!' I failed to reach him.

I even went so far as to get his parents' number from the phone book and I ended up speaking to his mother! She was probably my age or younger, and there was me – demented older woman wondering if her baby boy wanted to come out to play. Despite my best efforts, he never turned up.

And so the bitter tears of rage, loneliness, frustration and regret flowed freely once again and I had the devil's own job growing back the bits of me he stole while he was passing through.

People slide into your life like a knife and then withdraw – and not always cleanly...

♀

Some months later, out of the blue, Jake began emailing me from L.A. sending me photos of himself and excerpts from a film script he'd written. Memory being selective 'n all, I was of course thrilled to hear from him. I did give him a bit of a ruck for having stood me up that time, and he apologised profusely, saying something so personal had happened he couldn't possibly tell me what it was! Had his dick dropped off? Did he have a violent attack of diarrhoea in his pants on his way to meet me? Or was this just a giant cop-out as he couldn't think of anything better to say? Whatever...I forgave him and we maintained contact until his next trip back to London a few months later.

And so it came to pass that one Sunday evening in September, Wendy (now aged fifty-seven) found herself parked outside Finchley Road tube station awaiting the return of Peter Pan (still aged twenty-nine). This time he did me the great honour of keeping our appointment and hauled his cute little ass up my stairs once more. There was no delicious meal to eat – I wasn't going there again – but our reunion had nothing to do with what was in my fridge. We had each other to feast on and did so with relish and delight which brought the joy of sex back into my life and eliminated the bad taste left over from the time before. The restorative power of being worshipped by this young man, even for just a few hours, could not be underestimated and I still get a warm glow whenever I think of it.

On saying goodbye for what was probably the last time, he paid me the greatest compliment I have ever had. When I dropped him back at the station at 1 a.m., he took my face in his hands, smiled deeply into my eyes, kissed me hard on the lips and said:

'You're a GODDESS! It's as simple as that.'

And like that elusive dragonfly, he took off...back into his life.

WILLIAM

I LIKE OLDER MEN...

BUT I COULDN'T EAT A WHOLE ONE

To inject some stability into my social life, I do go out with older men, any one of whom, if I listened to my mother, I should hurry up and settle down with. Most are generous and charming, but the trouble is, when they take me out for dinner, all I want to eat is the waiter.

One of my suitable suitors is a man named William. We'd been introduced at a dinner party and although I was far from smitten, he had a certain *je ne sais quoi*. He was of the right demographic, status, class and intellect, and was well-travelled, cultured, erudite, entertaining and loaded. He always produced best seats for the theatre, ballet and opera, and a meal – whether before or after – was effortlessly enjoyed at one of London's top restaurants, where we'd saunter in sans reservation and get a table immediately. A whole house in Holland Park Avenue with 2.4 gardeners and a dog may be some girls' idea of heaven but it sounded to me like a slow comfortable death.

When it comes to ageing Lotharios, fending them off at the end of the evening is a delicate task, especially when you've accepted their hospitality. No one likes rejection – whether given or received – but the sad truth is that *men still expect sex in exchange for food*. They don't really want to be friends; they don't understand the meaning of the word 'platonic' and if you're not prepared to play ball(s) they'll find a woman who will. *I buy you dinner, you'll be dessert* is a very common expectation. One old fatty once said to me: 'I know I'll get you sooner or later' to which I replied: 'How do you feel about necrophilia?'

Having said all that, I do have some treasured old buddies whose company I thoroughly enjoy. OK, so they fall asleep in the theatre the minute the lights go down and the curtain goes up, and I've often had to nudge them awake to stop them from snoring, but that's the way we're all headed. And there is a certain comfort in being with one's own peer group. You don't have to worry about saying you saw the Beatles live then watch them doing the maths like a toyboy might.

Anyway, back to William...

William was more than a little overweight, balding, had a fleshy sack where his neck used to be and an occasional tic in his left eye. Despite a considerable fortune, he dressed like he'd been dipped in glue and thrown through the window of an Oxfam shop. Why would a man think un-pressed grey flannel trousers and a moth-eaten check jacket went perfectly well with a pair of trainers which looked like Fido had been feasting on them? There was no way I could take my cousin the counsellor's advice to 'close your eyes and think of Cartier'. I'm sorry – diamonds may be a girl's best friend, but there are limits... To William's credit, and to my despair, he never stopped trying, a typical example of how God gave men a brain and a penis but only enough blood to run one of them at a time.

And so, on that particular evening, William arrived to pick me up in his brand new silver BMW-convertible-prick-extension-thingy. This made him marginally more attractive, but still...no cigar. The minute he got the car into gear, he reached across and put his hand territorially on my thigh. I sighed deeply and tensed up, ignoring it in the hopes it would go away, and eventually it did.

The dinner party was another matter, as I recorded in my diary later that same night:

The minute I walked up the path of this stylish villa in the posh part of Islington I knew I was going to have to beat off the host (he'd have liked that!). As William and I strolled towards the house, this larger-than-life character bounded out of the undergrowth, shook Will's hand and scooped me up bodily in his arms.

'What have we here?' he boomed as if I were a new species of undiscovered mammal. He gave me a wet, sloppy kiss on both cheeks removing half my make-up, and dragged me into the house where he introduced me to his tetchy little wife who smiled tightly and went back to the kitchen. Not letting go of me for an instant, he whispered lasciviously: 'Let me show you where the fairies live' and next thing I know we're down the bottom of the garden and he's flashing his agapanthus at me. I managed to extricate myself before he got too amorous and hurried back to the safety of William's side and a very large V & T.

The wife was simpering in a much-put-upon kind of way, and there was a distinctly ratty dynamic going on between them. She'd obviously been stuck in the kitchen all day while he'd been down the wine cellar having a private tasting of all that was quaffable. By the time the guests arrived he was four sheets to the wind and she was hot, stressed and twitchy. Every time he opened his mouth to speak, she shot him an 'Oh, must you?' look and threw her eyes skywards to the Farrow & Ball Ecru Linen ceiling. By his nicotine-stained fingers and the size of his gut, you could see he was a bon vivant – had probably had a string of affairs and was up for another one asap. And there was me, the only single woman at a couples' dinner party, fair game for any fruity old married... or so he thought.

Over cocktails and canapés, he started the dangerous game of topping up my glass every time I took a sip, leaning over salivating like an old Labrador. When the conversation turned to antiques and my knowledge thereof, he whisked me off to his den to check out his George III bracket clock which he insisted had stopped chiming. I told him that clocks were not my area of expertise, but he was having none of it and pressed himself hard up against me as he showed me the mechanism. I certainly got him going...but sadly, not the clock.

We went in to dinner and I sat down at my place card. The wife came in carrying the soup tureen and stopped dead in her tracks.

'Oh! I see!' she said, glaring at me. Well he'd changed the bloody table plan, hadn't he? Not my fault. As soon as we were settled, he entwines his foot round mine and asks me how long I've known 'old Willy' for, which conjured up exactly the sort of image I'd been trying to avoid... When I answered 'About a year' he said 'Well he's kept you jolly quiet, hasn't he?' like he had every right to know.

'Maybe because there's nothing to tell...' I shot back and so the evening proceeded at a jolly pace. While wifey was clearing up the coffee things, I went to the loo which was situated across the oak-panelled hall at the back of a cupboard under the stairs. When I came out, mein host materialised like ectoplasm through the coats and, breathing boozily into my face, slobbered: 'I'd very much like to see you again...somehow?'

His eyes were bloodshot, his lips slack, hanging open in fulsome expectation. It was disgusting. I shrugged him off and moved back into the hallway, just as the others were exiting the dining-room. We said our thank-yous and goodbyes and left – him standing mournfully in the doorway like a boy whose new-found teddy was being carted off by the dustmen.

On the way home, I thought it only polite to thank William for a lovely evening to which he replied rather crisply: 'Yes! I noticed you flirting with Philip!'

'I rather think it was the other way round' I countered, 'and I couldn't very well blank the host, could I?'

Honestly, men – and in any case, Philip is a heart attack waiting to happen, and it's not going to happen on top of me.

♀

One Saturday afternoon some weeks later, I was sitting on the sofa doing some sewing when my phone rang.

'Wenday?' said a voice I didn't recognise.

'Y-yes?' I replied hesitantly.

'It's Philip Warwick.'

The long silence that ensued gave him enough time to realise I had no idea whom I was talking to.

'You came to my home for dinnah? A few weeks ago? With Willy-am?'

'Oh, yes...' I answered slowly, wondering how in hell he'd got my number 'How *are* you?'

'Very well,' he slavered. 'Actuallay...I'm in your road...'

Well nobody's 'in my road' unless they're invited to be so. It's not a main thoroughfare or even a cut-through. He'd made a special journey. The nerve of it!

I put on my most imperious voice and in a tone intended to embarrass him I replied:

'...*AND*...?'

'...and I thought I'd pop up and see you.'

It sounds like you've already 'popped up' you old dog, I thought.

'I'm sorry, Philip,' I retorted sternly, 'but it's not convenient nor am I receiving just now.'

'Oh...' he answered sheepishly, 'Alright then... Er...sorry to have troubled you.'

And he hung up.

I did feel a bit guilty, but what was he expecting? That a woman on her own was going to drop her knickers on a Saturday afternoon just because he happened to be in her road? Apart from which he'd never have made it up my stairs.

The arrogance of the penis never ceases to amaze me...

MATTHEW
MY BOY LOLLIPOP

The weekend in Barcelona held little promise except to escape the drizzly London weather and meet up with some old friends. I'd been invited to a wedding, but annoyingly I'd been invited on my own. I had no one special in my life at the time, but I could certainly have rustled up a dance partner or two. I asked the hostess if there'd be any single men there but the answer was 'Sorry, no...' – only loads of unattached women.

The prospect of entering couple kingdom as a single citizen is daunting, especially on social occasions like these. There's always the fear that everyone on your table will get up to dance and you'll be left sitting there with an 'I'm-really-enjoying-myself...NOT' smile pasted on your face.

I'm a good networker and knew a few people there so on arrival at the champagne reception I downed my first Bellini, scooped up another and set off in search of familiar faces.

There was a great ambience, much joy and congratulation being dispensed to the happy families by the well-heeled guests. The dinner was excellent, the atmosphere convivial, and with three interesting, single women at my table there was no shortage of good conversation, so the dreaded solo moment never arrived. The event turned into one big party and by midnight we were all on the dance floor strutting our stuff. I was surrounded by my table companions, the two-year-old pageboy, the eighty-year-old grandmother and the rest of the glamorous guests.

As I scanned the room, I noticed an abundance of tall, dark, handsome, young, male friends of the bride and groom's, their black ties and dinner jackets discarded as they danced to the music. I also observed their girlfriends and partners: tall, slim, cool, glamorous gazelles one and all. Much to my dismay, I felt invisible. This is the future, I thought and subliminally invoked the Good Fuck Fairy to look out for me.

The following day, a post-wedding lunch party had been arranged at a ranch house up in the hills. People had flown in from all over the world so the host family were thoughtful not to leave them high and dry after the nuptials. We congregated at the hotel at 2 p.m. A couple of coaches were on hand to take us up to the *finca* and as we waited for everyone to assemble I noticed some of the guests looking worse for wear from the night before.

Looking around, I spotted an attractive grey-haired woman being danced attendance upon by a gorgeous, dark-haired young man. He was wearing Ray-Bans, and occasionally rubbed his temple like he was nursing a hangover. He talked intimately to her, offering her a cigarette, lighting it and running to find an ashtray. They seemed very bonded, very together. Lucky cow, I thought. Is he her toyboy? I continued to observe them. He whispered something in her ear then left her side and came over to speak to a man standing near me. I didn't remember seeing this guy the night before, and wondered if he'd even been there. As I was pondering this thought, he looked straight at me, raised his sunglasses and stuck them on top of his head. Our eyes met and a flicker of interest flashed between us. Hmmm, I thought. Could be a fun afternoon...

We were called to board the coaches and he went back to accompany the woman. I sat down on an aisle seat and as he walked past me, our eyes met again. I turned casually to watch where he went and saw the woman sit down next to someone else. He proceeded to the back of the coach where he plonked himself down alone. Curiouser and curiouser, thought Alice as she tried not to rubberneck.

The lunch party was a fiesta of food, flamenco and *mucha sangria*. Fortuitously, the young man was right in my eye-line at the table opposite and, again, I saw him attending to the woman's every need: refilling her glass, passing her plates of *tapas*, whispering confidentially in her ear. He was also knocking back the booze at an alarming rate. So, it has to be said, was I.

'Who's that over there?' I asked the lady next to me, who seemed to know everyone.

'That's Marisa Truman,' she answered.

'With her...lover?' I enquired.

'Oh no, no, no!' she laughed. 'That's Matthew. Her son.'

'Oh!' I replied, and the gates of possibility swung open and I stepped through them into Maybeland.

'Is he...er...gay?' I queried tentatively. The thought had suddenly occurred to me.

'Not at all!' my neighbour answered. 'He's a very good son. She lost her husband a month ago...his father...they were very close. Actually, Matthew got married last year, but it broke up already...the girl ran off with his best friend...'

No wonder he looked wired and was drinking so much. And hanging on to Mummy for dear life.

The meal ended and the entertainment began. A noisy troupe of singers and dancers blazed onto the floor, castanets clacking, guitars thrumming. I'd studied flamenco for six years as a child and could barely sit still when I heard those gypsy rhythms. The heart-felt *cante* and the pulsing *palmas* and *zapateado* lifted me right out of my seat. I decided to go and stand at the bar where I could tap and clap to my heart's content without feeling self-conscious. I got up and weaved my way through the tables, ensuring that I passed Matthew en route. He was just lighting another cigarette.

'There's no smokers at my table,' I confided impulsively. 'Mind if I cadge one?' I'd have puffed a pipe full of moose manure if he'd offered it. He handed me a Marlboro and flicked open his Zippo. Our eyes met and held yet again.

'Thanks,' I breathed and sashayed over to the bar, wishing I had a magnet up my arse.

Apparently I did. He took the bait, whispered something to Mother, then got up and walked over to where I stood. My fishing rod was twitching furiously.

We started chatting and he asked me if I'd been at the wedding. Like I said, I'd been invisible!

'I didn't get in 'til six this morning,' he yawned. 'Some of us went out clubbing...'

'I wish I'd known,' I said. 'I'd have come too.' If I'd been invited.

'Maybe tonight?' he suggested. 'If we're not too knackered?'

'Maybe...' I replied, not wishing to sound too eager, my

mind shrieking 'Yes. Yes. What'll I wear?'

The cabaret ended and he gave me a wink and returned to his table. I went off to chat to the bride, feigning interest in Matthew for one of my daughters.

'He's a head case,' she told me. 'Lovely guy but not in a good place right now. His wife...'

'Yes I heard...' I cut in, now even more convinced he needed a nice, warm bosom to cry on.

When we got back on the coach, Matthew, without waiting to he asked, plonked himself right down next to me. Satisfaction was my middle name, especially when he allowed his leg to loll against mine. I didn't move away and the journey passed with us leaning tipsily against each other, whispering nonsense and exchanging deep and dirty looks.

Back at the hotel, most of the other guests drifted off to their rooms. A few of us went to the bar, including Matthew and I. I'd had more than enough to drink, but I wasn't going to let this one get away. He sat down next to me then abruptly got up again and walked off. My heart sank then rose when he returned a few moments later with something white clutched between his fingers. He checked no one was looking and motioned it towards me. It took me a moment to twig. I dropped my hand discreetly towards his and he pushed a piece of folded paper into it. I stifled a giggle, scrunched it up and nonchalantly continued my conversation. After a short interval, bursting with curiosity, I excused myself and strolled off as casually as I could towards the Ladies Room.

'Meet me in the gardens in 10 mins' it read. How deliciously decadent! I couldn't have planned this better if I'd tried! I powdered my nose and glossed my lips then found my way to the terrace doors. I checked behind me for any snoopers and slipped quietly out into the hotel grounds.

It was early evening and a few faraway stars were twinkling in the darkening sky. I looked around and saw Matthew in the shadows ahead of me He was leaning up against a tree by the swimming pool, one knee bent with his foot on the trunk: very sexy, very James Dean. All he needed was a Stetson pulled down low over one eye. Treading carefully so my heels wouldn't sink into the grass, I sauntered over and he immediately put his arms around my waist and pulled me against him. I tensed and looked around anxiously to check if we could be seen from the hotel bar.

'What's this all about?' I asked, feigning an innocence I did not possess. In reply I got the greatest chat-up line of all time.

'I think you ought to know...' he said slowly, slurring slightly yet savouring every syllable, 'that I have... *(pause for effect)*...the most.......enormous........COCK.'

The word was well-aimed and he shot it at me like a bullet. I mean, where's a girl to go with information like that? You can't just take it or leave it. You *have* to get involved.

I was rather shocked at this personal revelation and I blinked rapidly, my brain processing the powerful piece of knowledge. Matthew stood there with a self-satisfied smirk on his face. Well, he would, wouldn't he? As the implications sunk in, a lascivious smile curled the corners of my mouth. I almost had to stop myself from dribbling. I tried to temper my reaction not to flatter him too much but all my emotions were currently heading south. He continued to smirk. The cock was cocky, that's for sure.

'I only have your word for that,' I replied, trying to bring him down to size. 'And by whose standards anyway? Do you check out other men in the shower rooms?'

'No. Really,' he insisted. 'Feel this.'

And he grabbed my hand and parked it right on his groin. I snatched it back in alarm. Either he'd stuck an entire *chorizo* down his trousers or he was indeed telling the truth.

'Ohmigod!' I uttered, unable to mask my amazement. 'You're not lying!'

And he pulled me against him again and plunged his tongue deep into my mouth. There was no doubt in my mind. I had to see it. Touch it. Lick it. Taste it. Feel it. Have it.

'I'm going back to my room now,' I burbled, giving myself time to think. I was suddenly unable to breathe properly. 'Shall we meet back in the bar in an hour?'

'I'm sharing with my Mother,' he replied. 'I'll come to yours, shall I?'

'No you won't!' I answered, mortified at the suggestion. 'Someone might see us. The hotel's heaving with people I know. Anyway, who said anything about...?'

He raised one eyebrow mockingly at me. The futile rhetoric of my question vaporised in the evening mist. Who was I fooling? Certainly not him.

Matthew obviously used his dick as a passport. I imagine it got him into all sorts of places, but I didn't want to make it that easy for him. I extricated myself from his embrace and said: 'Nine o'clock. In the bar.'

And I teetered back across the lawn, my mind racing, my throat swelling, my stomach churning, my heart doing aerobatics in my chest. What a spectacular change of luck.

At 9.10 p.m. I was back in the bar chatting to some of the other guests when his mother walked in. She sat down next to me and we started talking. We ordered Virgin Marys which came with nuts, crisps and olives. She was very friendly and I was wondering what the hell I was going to do with her if and when her son turned up. In the event, I needn't have worried. 9.30 became 10 o'clock and still there was no sign of him. Conversation was running thin and I was beginning to agitate.

'I wonder where Matt has got to...' she said at long last, looking at her watch. I could have hugged her. My thoughts exactly!

'Are you having dinner together?' I asked, trying to gauge how the evening might pan out.

'I don't think so...' she answered and picked up her mobile phone to dial the room. There was no reply. Disappointment clutched at my heart. I swallowed hard wondering how long I could decently sit there waiting. She kept trying the room and eventually he picked up. She said a few words and then disconnected.

'He was asleep,' she said. 'In the bath. Silly boy. He'll be down soon.'

Hope leapt eternal. I took a long drink of water and nibbled absently on the nuts and olives. Conversation lumbered on like a Third World bus with two flat tyres. At 10.50 p.m. I decided enough was enough. Two hours of small talk was my upper limit and I was wound up, let down, mentally and physically exhausted. My neck was aching with tension and I'd practically ground my teeth down to the roots.

'I'm going up,' I said, doing some kind of fake yawn and stretch. 'Enjoy the rest of your evening. What time's your flight tomorrow?'

'Early,' she said vaguely. 'It doesn't seem like Mattie's going to come...' *(Moi non plus* I thought bitterly.) 'I may as well go up with you,' and we walked together across the reception hall.

The lift doors opened and there he stood. He looked from his mother to me and back again and I raised an eyebrow and pursed my lips. Great timing, tosser.

'Sorry,' he apologised to his mother, pecking her on the cheek. 'You going to bed? I'm just waking up!'

'That's because you've had a three-hour sleep,' she scolded.

'Oh come back to the bar,' he cajoled. 'Have a nightcap. I don't want to drink alone.'

'No, I'm tired,' she said and stepped into the lift.

I looked at my watch stalling for time.

'I'll keep you company,' I sighed like it was the greatest sacrifice on earth. 'But only a quick one.'

He gave me a telling look, kissed his mother again on the cheek, whispered 'Sleep well' and waited for the lift gates to close. He turned towards me grinning. I gave him my best 'You Bastard' look and headed back towards the bar, but he caught my arm.

'Let's go into town,' he said and frogmarched me back through reception and out onto the street.

We walked until we found a small *taberna* in an alleyway off *Las Ramblas*. We sat down and ordered *vino tinto* and he immediately began running his hand up and down my thigh. I was uncomfortable with this behaviour in public, but as we were the only people in there, it seemed churlish to make a fuss.

'While you were sleeping,' I told him once I'd begun to unwind a little, 'your mamma told me what a good boy you always were. Personally I think you're a very bad boy. And I wonder if when she was changing your nappy, she knew what a very big boy you were going to grow into!'

He sniggered. 'She's been a good friend to me... I've had a shit year what with my Dad and stuff. She's been my rock.'

No wonder he was so attentive towards her. She was his everywoman: Earth-Mother-Nature, the one female men worship the most, and the one they can never have.

As the wine relaxed him, Matt set about nuzzling my neck and nibbling my ear.

'What's your room number?' he whispered but I just giggled and shook my head.

'If you want me badly enough,' I teased 'you'll have to find an alternative venue...or wait until we get back to London.'

I fancied having him to look forward to. *He* was obviously living in the moment.

'Come on,' he said abruptly, having come to a decision. He threw some euros on the table, got up and with focused determination weaved me smartly across the road and into the grand marble hallway of Le Méridien Hotel.

'Do you have a suite available for one night?' he asked the receptionist confidently, placing his credit card down on the counter with a smart click.

I admired his style but moved away, embarrassed by the fact that I was checking into a top hotel in the middle of the night with a man half my age and no luggage. I stood staring at the glittering array in the Bulgari showcase, listening to the transaction taking place. Matthew got the key card, turned from the desk and smoothly swept me along with him towards the lifts. We were kissing and giggling when the doors opened on the eighth floor. I escaped and ran along the corridor with him in hot pursuit until we found our suite. We burst in like a couple of kids, and ran around exploring the living-room, kitchen, bathroom, dressing-room, terrace and finally, the bedroom with its king-sized bed. Matthew raided the mini-bar and brought two small vodkas over to where I stood. We cracked the tops off and swigged them down in one. He took my bottle from me and lobbed them both accurately into the waste bin.

'Shall I go halves with you on this?' I offered, my tongue burning from the fiery spirit. 'You needn't have...'

He shook his head and with effortless ease, scooped me up like a bride and plonked me down right in the middle of the great big bed. He bounced on beside me and started to unpeel my clothing. I came up to kneeling, panting with anticipation at what was to come.

I unbuttoned Matthew's shirt and he shrugged it off. His naked torso revealed broad shoulders, well-defined pecs, a narrow waist and a rippling six-pack leading down to a fine line of silky brown hair which beckoned temptingly from the top of his jeans. I leaned over and flipped the bedside light switch off so the room became soft and muted, a flattering glow wafting in gently from the living-room. I lowered my gaze inquiringly down to his crotch and back up again to meet his eyes.

'Well?' I provoked. 'Let's see it then!'

With a flick of his wrist, Matthew flipped open the top button of his jeans and lowered the zip tantalisingly one tooth at a time. That self-satisfied smile spread again across his face. My heart was flapping in my chest like a bird against a windowpane and I was almost afraid to look now the moment of truth had actually arrived. Very slowly, I lowered my glance and there, poking its swollen head at least four inches above the parapet, was a tumescence of such girth and magnitude it fair took my breath away. I stared hard, gawping open-mouthed, and I couldn't help but gasp in shock and admiration. I licked my index finger and ran it slowly around the rim. I reached forward and lowered the rest of the zip taking care not to catch his pubic hair. The Penis sprang forth, bobbed heavily this way and that and came to rest centre stage pointing directly at me.

Wheel of Fortune! I grasped it firmly in my hand and my fingers did not meet around it. I pushed it flat up against his stomach. It reached well past his navel. It was indeed A Most Enormous Cock.

Matthew must have revelled in this moment – and all the times he'd experienced it before and since. He knew exactly what it provoked: an inevitable and inexorable desire for the woman concerned to sink her lips over it and see how far she could take it in her mouth. It was the ultimate dummy, a giant lollipop, a fantasy sex tool – verily a dish to set before a king (or queen in the case of Dame Elton John).

Matthew was a horny bastard and once we got started, he wanted to do all sorts of things I simply could not accommodate. We thrashed and trashed the king-size bed in a frenzy of hot, raw, rampant sex until we were both sweat-soaked and dripping with the exquisite effort of it all.

Later, as we lay resting, I played with his pendulous flaccidity and it came back to life once more. I watched it rise and marvelled how God had indeed been generous. The next guy in the queue obviously got zilch. What I took away from this experience (apart from the inability to walk for two days) was the conviction that, despite what anyone says, Size Does Matter. My only regret was not having had a camera handy because when I related the story to my girlfriends, like a fisherman, there was no way any of them were going to believe me.

A couple of weeks later, back in Blighty, I was in the cinema with a group of buddies when my mobile began to vibrate in my handbag. I grabbed it anxiously, wondering if a daughter or my mother had a problem at 10.20 p.m. on a Saturday night. To my utter surprise, it was a text from Matthew asking if I was free. I'd never expected to hear from him again! I scrambled out of my seat, treading on everyone's toes as I went, and ran up the aisle to the exit. I texted him back affirmative, returned to my friends, whispered that I didn't feel well and drove home like Michael Schumacher being chased by a bear in a Ferrari.

I freshened up, lit some candles, put on some music, opened a bottle and the doorbell rang. This dude wasted no time. He entered my flat, pecked me a brief hello, looked left and right then marched straight through into the bedroom. He yanked open the door to my dressing-room and started rifling through my shoe collection. The best ones are kept neatly stacked in boxes and they were soon strewn all over the floor. He selected the lilac suede LK Bennetts with the gold ankle strap and killer heels and threw them down at my feet. I obediently put them on and strutted around the room while he assessed the effect. Mission accomplished, he threw me onto the bed and off we went.

This shoe fetish became a ritual the next few times he came to call and I even bought a pair of black patent whore's platform stilettos just for his visits. He'd always arrive in a state of grubby insouciance, unshaven, in combats or faded jeans and I was always dolled up to the nines. I didn't care. This guy could have had any woman he wanted...a Porfirio Rubirosa of our times.

Matthew with his sex-god endowment was a rare blessing, so whoever up there engineered it for me, thank you very much.

By the way, can anyone tell me how *Memento* ended?

JAMES
PREMATURE INFATUATION

If you ever happen to be ambling through the streets of Mayfair you will come across an assortment of art galleries, each one plying their wares to the rich and suggestible. Mostly the exhibits are nothing you would want to share houseroom with, but if you enter, browse and make appreciative noises, you will be asked to sign the Visitors' Book. This will entitle you to receive a series of embossed invitations to Private Views until the Gallery goes bankrupt or their lease runs out - whichever is the sooner.

One Thursday evening, with not a lot else to do, I perused the stiffies reclining on my mantelpiece. One was for 'A Collection of Works Studying the Dynamics of Line, Form and Texture' by a new artist who'd been voted the 'One to Watch' in the Culture Section of the *Sunday Times*. My motto being 'Exposure Equals Opportunity', I decided to take the opportunity to expose myself. I dressed up, drove into town and parked my car in Burlington Gardens. I sauntered along Cork Street like a woman with a purpose and soon I came to number twenty-seven. You need a certain amount of bottle to barge into a gathering of complete strangers and mingle, but I pasted on my most confident smile, pushed open the heavy glass door and entered the fray.

The freeloaders stood shoulder-to-shoulder inside the brightly-lit gallery quaffing Cava and ignoring the installations which ranged from the reclined to the vertiginous. God helps those who help themselves, so I helped myself to a glass from the tray proffered by the rented waiter in the ill-fitting tux and raised my antenna to scan the room. I smiled and nodded at an elderly dowager I'd seen before at such events, and as the woman moved away in search of canapés, I spotted a group of suits standing chatting just behind her. I studied them one by one but they held little interest: grey businessmen 'working late at the office' to delay the suburban journey home. I roamed around the gallery stopping intermittently to scrutinise the exhibits, my eyes and ears checking left and right.

The main door opened and closed as people departed and others came in. A group of giggling office girls entered and on their heels a toweringly tall, sharply-chiselled young man. My antenna quivered with interest and curiosity. I took a sip of my fizz, watched and waited. He picked up a glass and looked around. He was not with the gigglers as I'd originally thought, but appeared to be on his own and was clearly uncomfortable and seemed out of place. He began to wander aimlessly around the gallery, then stopped to study a sheet of brushed steel threaded with strips of coloured organza forming the outline of a naked woman. He looked to be around thirty and was wearing stone-washed chinos, a beige polo neck, a brown leather jacket and suede shoes. He had a laptop case tucked under one arm. He stood head and shoulders above anyone else, his endless legs rising all the way up to his brains. He had a well-defined profile, aquiline nose, strong jaw and toffee-brown hair combed back over a broad, unlined forehead. The whole look said Hugo Boss model with an Oxbridge degree.

I prowled towards him like a panther approaching a grazing gazelle and stood within sensing distance pretending to appraise the same work of art. He became aware of my presence and I glanced up at least a foot into his olive-green eyes. In close-up, his film-star good looks were quite startling.

'Hel-low' I said, all my allure centred in that one sound. 'Seen anything that appeals?'

'I have now,' he answered, giving me the once over. He raised one finely-arched eyebrow and lifted his glass in salute.

'Wendy Salisbury,' I smiled, swapping my drink into my left hand and extending my right one towards him.

'James Hammerson-Drake,' he replied, crushing my hand in the full force of his masculine grip. My amethyst and diamond ring stabbed painfully into the adjoining fingers.

'Aaow!' I winced as I reclaimed my crushed extremity and clasped it to my chest.

'Oh sorry!' he apologised. 'I didn't mean to...' and he took my hand back into his and examined it for injury.

'No harm done, I hope?' and he turned it over and placed a delicate peck on the open palm.

I was rather taken aback by this continental gesture and retrieved my hand swiftly. James smiled a satisfied smile as if he was pleased to have shocked me.

'So what do you do when you're at home?' he asked, suavely whisking another two glasses off a passing tray.

'I'm rarely *at* home,' I replied, accepting the second glass. 'I'm a freelance consultant in interior styling with collectibles and antiques,' and I reached into the side pocket of my handbag for one of my ever-ready business cards.

James studied the card closely and did that engaging eyebrow-raise once again.

'Which entails?' he asked.

'Offering creative advice on the purchase of antiques for investment to people who have the money but neither the time nor the nous to do it themselves.'

'Fancy...' he commented slipping the card into his top pocket.

Yes I do actually, I thought.

'And what do you do?' I enquired, entering into the social spirit dictated by such occasions.

'Also creative....er...director. Ad agency.'

'Mmmm...interesting...' I lied, taking another sip of the wine. 'And what brings you here tonight? Business or pleasure?'

'Actually...' James confessed after a momentary pause. 'Neither. I'm afraid I'm a fraud.'

'Like most of the people here, I would imagine,' I commented.

'I've just come from a job interview,' he went on. 'Creative Director in an ad agency is what I'd like to be. I'm working my way up the food chain. Right now I'm plankton. I was on my way home when I saw the buzz and smelt the booze. Thought I could blend in and grab a free snifter without being rumbled.'

He gave a self-conscious little laugh which didn't quite match his stature.

'What's it worth not to tell?' I joked, glad to have him in

my confidence. 'It must be a bit difficult to blend in when you're...how tall?'

'6'4½".'

'Wow!' I said. Your legs are going to stick right off the end of my bed.

We small-talked London for a while and I found out all I needed to know. James was a charmer, bright and educated but potless, single and living in a shared rental in Tooting. None of which affected my life one iota.

The crowd began to thin and we drifted towards the exit. I told James to sign the Visitors' Book so he'd get regular invitations and as he did so, I looked over his shoulder and memorised his email address. We left the gallery together and hovered around outside. He seemed to be waiting for me to say something. In true showbiz tradition, I decided to leave him wanting more.

'It's been lovely meeting you,' I said, holding out my hand then quickly retrieving it.

'Whoops!' I laughed. 'Not going there again.'

'What...about...' he hesitated, '...maybe a drink sometime?'

'Sure,' I said casually. 'You've got my card.'

I reached up to pat his top pocket. 'Oh, and good luck with the job hunt,' and I stood on tiptoe to kiss him goodbye. God, his skin...

James gave me a little wave, turned on his heels and set off with long strides towards the station. As I walked back to my car I licked my index finger and drew a 1 in the air.

The next morning, to my surprise, I received an email from him. He was clearly dyslexic as his spelling was atrocious but he opened up the lines of communication which, over the next couple of weeks, turned into a pretty, witty, daily repartee. It's strange how you can get so close to someone without ever seeing or touching them. Anyone who has internet dated will know this – the language can become quite intense and of course your imagination does the rest. Each email acted like a mini-date so you build some sort of relationship out of nothing. Although James and I had at least met, we were little more than strangers but through his emails I got to know him better, enough to know I'd feel safe seeing him again. Plus, of course, he was stunningly good-looking so even if he'd been a complete dork, he would at least have fitted one of my criteria. (Shallow? *Moi*?)

Although his writing was jokey and flip, he confided his job hunt problems to me and I gave him all the support I could. I try to combine 'experienced older woman' with 'hippy chick' so they don't feel threatened. It kids me that we're equal. We're not of course. To them I'm just another conquest, and to me they're just feathers I'm collecting to stuff a pillow with – a pillow I'll probably smother myself with one day.

James hadn't suggested meeting again but I steered the conversation around to likes and dislikes – favourite films, food – that sort of thing. He told me he hated onions, liver and cottage cheese so I suggested cooking for him 'sometime', promising not to make my signature dish of braised liver and onions with a dollop of cottage cheese on the side. To my pleasure, he accepted and when I threw him some possible dates, he opted for the following Saturday night. I found this choice very significant and the rest of the week passed in a blur of menu planning and gourmet shopping. Sometimes I have the memory of a goldfish. Or maybe I'm just an eternal optimist.

On the Saturday afternoon, he texted me. When I saw his name on my mobile screen, my heart took a dive, afraid the message would begin: Sorry but...

I'd done my usual big number: the food, the wine, the scented candles, the soft music...me...

Want 2 meet in yr local 4 a drink before diner(sic) he wrote.

I beg your pardon!? What *was* he on about? No I did not want to meet in my local for a drink before 'diner'. I didn't even understand the question. I mean, if a hot woman is waiting for you in the warmth of her elegant home what the hell are you doing suggesting meeting in a noisy, sweaty, smoky, skanky pub? Or maybe this was a territorial thing: he wanted to be in his comfort zone – I wanted to be in mine.

Got everything we need here including your Bombay Sapphire! I texted back. He'd professed a fancy for this particular tipple.

Then as an afterthought I wrote: ...everything but the boy...

To my surprise, he actually arrived on time. I live in a mansion flat with no lift and depending on their state of fitness, it can take visitors up to five minutes to reach my third floor flat. During this time, I usually put on the music, dim the lights and have a final titivate. James, being such a daddy-long-legs, bounded up the stairs at the speed of light, and suddenly there he was, standing on my threshold with the ubiquitous bottle of wine. I was rather dumbstruck when I saw him again. He looked like he'd been sent over by Central Casting to fill the role of 'tall, dark, handsome stranger.' He was illegally handsome, unfathomably tall and for as long as it lasted, irrevocably mine.

I hadn't drunk gin for years. When I was about eleven, I used to raid my father's cocktail cabinet and swig the

Gordon's from the bottle. He eventually rumbled me and took to locking the door and hiding the key. When I found it and opened the cabinet again, I saw he'd marked the bottle.

I poured two tumblers of Bombay and topped them up with tonic and lots of ice and lemon. We clinked glasses and drank. James then started roaming uninvited around my flat. What was it with these guys? This one was the nosiest bugger I'd ever met. He commented rather rudely on everything, opening drawers and cupboards and scrutinising the contents, picking things up and putting them back again in the wrong place. He examined the interior of my fastidiously furnished doll's house and mocked the miniature family residing within.

'He's a ging-er!' he howled, picking up the little son of the household. 'How can you give house room to a ging-er?' and he dropped the tiny red-haired doll onto the floor.

I retrieved it crossly and placed it back on the chair in the doll's house nursery. Then I closed the front of the house firmly and stood with my back against it. I leaned forward to smack James playfully on his hand but he caught me by the wrist causing me to yowl, and I started punching him in the stomach with my other hand. We ended up having a bit of a wrestle. This was a lost cause from the start and I collapsed in tipsy giggles which he exacerbated by tickling me in the ribs. I was getting quite drunk by this time and I had to perform a serious pelvic floor lift and beg for mercy for fear of wetting myself. He eventually let go of me and topped up our glasses, with a lot more gin than tonic. The evening was taking its natural course.

During our dinner of home-made gazpacho followed by mushroom, rocket and parmesan risotto, he told me all about his travels in India. He was an entertaining raconteur and the stories made me want to jump on the next flight to Mumbai. Not as a backpacker, of course; I rather fancied being carried through Rajasthan on a litter like some Victorian lady explorer. As I listened, I feasted my eyes on him, wondering why such a gorgeous hunk had chosen to grace *my* kitchen table on a Saturday night.

After dinner, as I was clearing the table, he lifted me onto the worktop alongside the sink. I felt a bit girly sitting there but it did bring us to approximately the same height. He then lunged clumsily at me and stuck his tongue down my throat. This approach did nothing whatsoever to turn me on. He began groping at my clothing, his hands a blur of activity as he fumbled to lift my top and lower my trousers all at the same time. I managed to extricate myself from this gauche attempt at seduction and jumped down.

'James! James...' I said as calmly as I could, my mini-stature putting me at a distinct disadvantage. 'Let's just take it a little bit slower, shall we?'

I sat him back down at the kitchen table and slowly straddled him. I ran my moistened lips lightly and sensuously across his. He immediately opened his mouth wide, his tongue waving around in search of mine. I drew away and closed his mouth with my thumb and forefinger.

'Less is more...' I whispered and kissed him again my way. He got the message and followed my lead as I teased my tongue very slowly against his, suckling his lips lightly to teach him the pleasure of prurience. The slow eroticism weaved its magic and I was now feeling really turned on. I led him into the living-room and we sat down on the couch. I leant my head back against the cushions offering him my naked throat. He kissed my neck and worked speedily down towards my cleavage dragging at my top and bra as he began to gnaw on my nipple.

'Gently Jamie...' I pleaded. 'Gently...' and he eased the pressure and obeyed my request.

Suddenly without warning, he stood up, lifted me bodily off the couch and planted me against him. I hugged my legs around his waist. I could feel his rigid hardness through his chinos as he jogged me up and down. He then strode across the room and dropped me rather ineptly onto the floor in front of the fireplace. He knelt beside me and undid my trousers and I raised my hips and wriggled out of them. He undid his own, let them drop and lay down on top of me in standard missionary position. He was wearing black jersey boxer shorts and with no further foreplay, he started to dry hump me urgently, moving hard and fast, one hand fumbling down towards his lowered jeans, presumably searching for a condom. He stopped abruptly, gasped, groaned, stiffened and jerked against me. I looked up at him not quite believing what had just happened. His lips were drawn tightly across his teeth. He rolled off me, cursed under his breath, and lay there staring up at the ceiling.

'It's OK...' I said indulgently. 'We can go again...' and despite my annoyance, I snuggled towards him, took his hand and put it down inside my panties.

I felt some resistance from him. Men, once they've ejaculated, wish immediately to be somewhere else. I was having none of that. Leaving him no choice, I got hold of his middle finger and used it for my own ends. In less than twenty seconds, we were even. Another notch on the bedpost...or in this case, the living-room floor.

James stood up wordlessly, pulled his jeans back on and went to the bathroom. I tidied myself up. The earlier excitement having hit pay dirt, there was nowhere left for the evening to go. On my list of Great Sexual Events of Our Time, this one would be placed firmly at the bottom.

He emerged fully dressed and looked at me as if he'd never seen me before. The magic had disappeared like Paul Daniels on a bad night. James was not a man for hugging, cuddling or kissing. There was no conversation left to be had and he clearly couldn't wait to leave. Declining my offer of coffee or anything else, he pecked me dryly on the cheek, mumbled 'Thanks for dinner' and departed.

My mood sank rather low as I cleared up, compounding the travelling and arriving theory.

♀

James had the grace to send me a thank-you email on the Monday morning, followed by a ten-day silence. I was miffed. I'd have done better to admire him from afar than spoil the illusion with too much reality. Then he emailed me again to say he'd found a job and suggested meeting up to celebrate. OK, I justified. Why not? Maybe he was just nervous that first time, and we had had a lot to drink. And, as eye candy, he was the whole store.

He came over on a week night and I threw together a quick pasta. We went to bed this time but he was still clueless, with no knowledge of the female body and even less interest in learning. He kept pushing my head down which is my absolute *bête noire*. I'll go down of my own free will and generally *only* if it's done to me first! Before we'd even got started, like the first time, he climaxed all over the place at which point I gave up. I actually felt a bit sorry for him...such a gorgeous, young specimen and yet...I'd had better sex with my Rabbit.

I got up and disappeared into my ensuite for the longest time. He took the hint and when I came out he was gone.

Oh well...I thought, as I put clean linen on the bed. You can't win 'em all!

WHERE'S THE WABBIT?

There are times when I've gone for months without sex and it hasn't really bothered me. If I'm reading a horny book or watching a sexy film, I get a natural twinge which I deal with in the usual way.

In the lulls between adventures or, as some people refer to them, 'relationships', I retreat into the warm comforting bosom of my family and the Sisterhood. My girlfriends are my rocks; there to cling to when the maelstrom gets too much, and no man, however fucking fabulous (it won't last) could possibly come between me and my homies. The dynamic between us is vibrant: a forceful flow of female energy so electric it would shock any bloke who dared to touch the fuse wire. Historically, we are likely to survive our men, and have in place contingency plans for the future. Gabriel García Márquez said: 'The secret of a comfortable old age is to make a pact with solitude.' Now solitude, and even singledom, is fine - but loneliness is not. So a group of us are thinking of selling our respective homes, pooling our resources and buying one big house together.

The plan is to employ Chippendales to cook, clean and garden while wearing little more than fake tan and a smile. There'll be an in-house health spa and casino where we can never lose and we'll keep fit with yoga, Pilates, salsa, tango and massage, and the staff (*Oxford English Dictionary:* sta:f/ stick, pole, rod...!) will be on hand to entertain us round the clock for the price of their bed and board. We'll have a master *chocolatier* and *patissier* in the kitchen, and more importantly, an in-house sex shop fully stocked with all the latest gadgets.

♀

I came late to the joy of sex toys, always preferring to get my kicks from live flesh rather than the Ann Summers variety. In the course of life's ups and downs, however, there are feasts and there are famines. When a frustrating episode like James crosses my path, better and more fulfilling sex can be achieved with the aid of a battery-operated gizmo specifically designed for the purpose.

In this context, I would like to pay tribute to the inventors of one particular tool, which is so knee-quiveringly, hip-raisingly, buttock-clenchingly, earth-movingly fantasmagorical, it has earned its name as every girl's must-have accessory. It is called the Rabbit.

The Rabbit is a contraption so wondrous it leaves its users catatonic in the nicest possible way. Save for the cuddle factor or the occasional need to get a lawn mown – not an issue for flat dwellers like myself – it actually makes men totally redundant. For how in heaven could a mere, masculine mortal simply endowed with two hands, one tongue and one penis be expected to electrify, gratify and satisfy in the way the Rabbit does? No matter the male's prowess, he could not possibly be gifted enough to synchronise his movements to such a pitch as to cause reliable multiple orgasms time after time. Plus, the user has complete control and autonomy over speed, placement, pressure and pleasure and even under the most dominant of direction, no poor bloke could ever compete with that.

But I digress... Rabbit users do that a lot...

Back to the story.

MRS ROBINSON SEEKS
BENJAMIN

In the lull between escapades, when my social pendulum
resumes a more regular swing, I still find myself yearning
for the thrill of a new chase. I get twitchy and bored
very easily – when you've been on a high, you want that
feeling to continue and the only way is to Make Something
Happen. Although I am content enough seeing friends or
spending the occasional evening vegged out in front of the
telly, much of the time I hanker after another adventure.

One evening I decided to seek some action by placing
a personal ad in the *Telegraph*. Toyboys had been thin on
the ground and short of hanging around the school gates, I
needed to conjure up a way of replenishing my stock. Like
any addiction, mine needs feeding and so I penned the
following ad:

Mrs Robinson seeks Benjamin. It's official, older women are in. Sophisticated, self-sufficient, slender siren seeks smart, secure, self-confident sugar baby to sweeten her life.

After a long rambling instruction from Ms Listen-Very-Carefully-and-I'll-Talk-You-Through-It, I read out the advert and recorded my voice message with a seductive huskiness not altogether my own.

Hello boys,

First let me compliment you on your good taste in answering this ad. If you think you're man enough to impress a quality lady and boy enough to qualify as eye and arm candy, then you've come to the right place. I am a mature, erudite, stylish, green-eyed blonde so if you are aged up to 38, tall, bright, entertaining and self-confident, give me a call. Oh...and most importantly, you've got to be gorgeous...so we match.

(I heard somewhere that self-confidence is a turn-on, though sometimes I feel I ought to be turned off.) Thank God there was a re-record option because this little piece of personal PR did not come easily. When I was just about satisfied I hadn't made a complete prawn of myself, I pressed the Save button, hung up and took stock. My heart was beating rather fast. I felt utterly wanton and mildly deranged, yet full of fizzy expectation. Looking back I may just as well have said:

'Sex-crazed senior seeks horny hunk NOW!'

I went to bed that night thinking: Sweet Mother, what *have* I done?

The paper came out the following Friday. I popped to the newsagents to buy a copy and sat on a nearby bench to scan the ads. I was shocked to actually see mine in print. It made me feel naked and exposed, like I'd gone out with no clothes on. I hurried home with my head bowed, the paper gripped firmly beneath my arm, imagining net curtains twitching as the locals pointed me out as the Whore of Babylon and muttered resentfully 'There goes the neighbourhood.'

Later that evening I dialled the 0906 retrieval number. Shock! Horror! I had SEVEN messages: Lucky Seven! The Magnificent Seven! The Seven Deadly Sins! The Secret Seven! The Seven Samurai! The Seven Dwarfs! Seven-Up? I sat on the edge of my bed, pressed 3 to listen and let the entertainment commence.

The first applicant had a soft, breathy voice, and sounded shy but rather engaging. The problem was he was a Glaswegian and I could only make out one word in ten of what he was saying. I moved swiftly on to number two who was very direct and asked if I wanted to 'meet up tonight for a swift half' and then I think I heard him whisper 'Fancy a fuck?' Well, yes, but...

The third applicant stuttered: 'I'm D-d-d-avid. C-c-c-call me' and left his mobile number which I tried to write down but it seemed to contain too many digits.

Out of the seven there were four I liked: Robert, Steve, Alan and Ozzie. I decided to call Steve straight away. He'd left a chatty, informative voice mail, and sounded normal and friendly. He said he was thirty-nine (a bit old for a Benjamin) and worked as a lawyer. Hmmm. I dialled his mobile number and he answered after the first ring which completely threw me as I hadn't thought beyond that point.

'Is this a good time to talk to Mrs Robinson?' I asked in as casual a voice as I could muster. He mumbled something about just leaving work and could he call me later? I said I'd ring him. I wasn't about to start handing out my phone

number willy nilly (unless the willy was irresistible).
Talking of willies, I had no idea where I was going with all
this (straight to the clap clinic probably!), but the upside
was I felt a buzz I hadn't felt in quite a while.

I tried to get a grip by doing some yoga, but despite stretching,
breathing, ohm-ing and standing on my head for as long
as I could balance, my mind just galloped forward to all
the delightful possibilities my ad had drummed up. I called
Steve again at 8 p.m. and found, after all, that he sounded
a bit jaded, like he'd played this game before. He gave me a
brief résumé of his life which was hardly inspirational and
we talked about the Mrs Robinson/Benjamin scenario. I
assured him I was neither a lush nor a sexual predator and,
call me naïve, but it hadn't occurred to me that that was
what I sounded like and what the responders expected. I
avoided the subject of age, banking on the combination of
their imagination and my mature allure coming together in
some kind of logic. Steve said he very much enjoyed the
company of older women and promised to email me his
photo the next day. He joked that he would have to get
his secretary to do it without arousing her suspicion and
it would probably be a holiday snap. Ooh! I might get to
see him in his Speedos! I promised to send mine by return.
Talking to him was nice enough but it didn't exactly get my
knickers twitching...

My next call was to Robert. I felt at ease with him
immediately. He was posh and funny and full of flattery,
saying my ad jumped off the page at him. Well, that was the
plan, Stan. I told him he sounded like Nigel Havers and he
admitted to having been mistaken for Hugh Grant or, on a
bad day, John Hurt. He can't organise a photo not having
access to a computer (Hallo?) but we got on really well,

so I decided to meet him anyway. He lives in Clapham but that's his problem. He admits to forty, so way over the hill for a toyboy, but he was erudite and suave in a thespy sort of way. When I declined to give him my age, he asked me if I was in my sixties!! Bloody cheek! Then it occurred to me that maybe he was looking for someone in their sixties...

I went to bed feeling happy and excited. Imagine how many people one would never meet without being a little proactive.

Steve's holiday picture came through next morning. Like my Jewish grandmother used to say when she couldn't get the right kind of fish for the *gefilte*: 'Oy! Voz ay-ee disappoint-ted!?' He had a curiously *retroussé* nose (not a good look in a man), a very long upper lip, sticky-out ears and hair which was not so much wavy as waving...goodbye! Poor love. Even in his youth, he was never a Benjamin, and he certainly wasn't one now. It was hard to reply without a putdown, but I emailed back with a comment about the lovely sandy beach and the castle in the background and tried to avoid saying anything else. Luckily he's going away for two weeks so by the time he gets back and maybe contacts me again, I could just say I'm dead or married or I've given it all up for Lent or something. Call me superficial, but no eye candy, no party.

On the Sunday, Robert called me six times between noon and 3 p.m. to arrange where and when to meet. We eventually settled on the Leinster Pub in Notting Hill at 4 p.m. When I walked in at five past, I knew him straight away. He was nursing a pint whilst looking expectantly at the door. He smiled when he saw me and although I smiled back I really wanted to turn on my heel and head home.

He certainly looked haggard for forty. He was obviously a heavy drinker, and impoverished to boot. He'd travelled halfway across London by public transport. I was looking for a knight on a white horse not an afternoon on a red bus.

The pub was full of football fans watching the Newcastle–Chelsea game. Robert probably gave the game and me equal attention and I sat there sipping a tomato juice wondering how soon I could decently get away. Chelsea were 3-0 up by half-time which prompted a rush to the bar giving me the chance to reflect on my stupidity. I'd missed a Pilates class and pretty much wasted my entire Sunday. That would teach me to check them out better in future and GET PHOTOS.

I left the pub at the beginning of the second half saying I had to visit my mother. Robert's eyes flickered between me and the TV screen but he did have the decency to stand up, shake hands and peck me goodbye. His hand felt dry and crisp like the last leaf of autumn and I felt rather sorry for him. He knew he wasn't going to see me again. I gave him the old 'Let's keep in touch' and went out into the darkening evening feeling doubtful and dejected.

When I got home there was a newcomer on the scene – Josh, aged 27! Now that's more like it, I thought, encouraged by his youth. I needed an antidote to unattractive Steve and sad, old Robert so I called Josh back straight away. He sounded a little timid but confessed immediately to being permanently turned on by the thought of an older woman. I pictured myself dressed as Mae West drawling: 'Is that a pistol in your pocket or are you just pleased to see me?'

We had a bit of a flirt on the phone and because he

sounded rather cute, I forgot my resolution to GET PHOTOS and cut straight to the chase. We agreed to meet for coffee on Tuesday afternoon.

Over the next few days I received loads more messages. The good stuck out a mile; the bad and the ugly got a polite rejection, and anyone lewd, crude or overtly rude got a smack round the chops. My evenings were totally taken up with listening to the voicemails, cataloguing them in order of preference and psyching myself up to calling them back. It was extremely time-consuming, hugely entertaining and totally addictive. I realised that I didn't actually need to meet any of them, so fulfilled was I with all this attention. It proves that women are just like flowers and a little water goes a long way.

There was Alan, who said he wanted to be naughty and could I lead him astray? I imagined myself dressed up St Trinian's-style sucking a lollipop while sticking my bum in his face. We emailed back and forth a couple of times, but he claimed not to know how to scan and send a photo. For God's sake, I'm a grandmother and I can do it. What is it with these guys?

Another contender was Ozzie, one of the original seven. He was very keen, and had called me twice. I texted his mobile and asked him to email me his photo, which he did, by return. He looked very rugged and outdoorsy with blue-eyes and blond hair. He was dressed in jeans and a check shirt, his Timberland-clad foot resting on a tree stump. Had me humming 'I'm a lumberjack...' straight away. He used to be a Naval Officer. He wasn't bad-looking but would probably want to go white-water rafting on our first date, and I don't go anywhere that doesn't have a fully-stocked dressing-table and a marble ensuite.

Then there was Arrogant Andrew whose voicemail went like this:

I AM your Graduate. You WILL know me. I am looking for discreet mental and physical intercourse where our minds and bodies can merge. Once you have tried me, you won't WANT anyone else.

What a tosser! He left me his mobile number so for a laugh I texted him to send me his photo. Later that evening I was having a pre-dinner drink with one of my suitables in the bar of the Institute of Directors in Pall Mall, when he texted me back:

Im on your screen now. So what do you think? as if I'd been sitting in front of my laptop for the past four hours waiting for him to manifest. I found him intensely annoying and he definitely needed pulling down a peg. He sounded like the type who'd ask you what you thought of his performance before, during and after sex. I decided to ignore him, which provoked so many self-aggrandising texts I had to switch my phone off.

♀

On the Tuesday morning, before meeting baby Josh, I went to have my highlights done. I go to the Greenhouse in Wigmore Street which is neither over-priced nor pretentious, but is sometimes frequented by celebrities. I was in a very good mood and sitting next to me in the salon was a divine, young guy who could have been in a boy band. I was aware that my body language was pitched at him noticing me, and then I caught sight of myself in the mirror. I saw a middle-aged woman with a head full of silver foils like a space traveller from a 1950s sci-fi movie. She was wearing a black nylon cloak which went from her neck to her knees and a pair of half-specs perched on the end of her nose. She may have felt eighteen but in that garb she looked plain and ridiculous. I shrunk down in my seat and stuck my alien head back between the pages of Italian *Vogue*.

♀

In the afternoon, blondied and beautified, the remains of my crayfish and rocket sandwich duly removed from between my teeth, I set off for Sloane Square to meet Josh, the baby of all the Benjamins.

There were three or four guys hanging around outside the station and one of them was the most drop-dead stunning example of manhood I have ever seen. I slowed my pace and hung back to observe him. His hair was long and slicked back off his forehead, continental-style. It was a rich shade of chestnut streaked with natural gold. He had deeply-tanned olive skin, a perfectly straight nose, full succulent lips and eyes the colour of jade fringed by the longest of lashes. He was utterly exquisite, probably Italian, and if he *was* Josh, I was prepared to convert to Catholicism. All thoughts of other Benjamins momentarily arrested, I drifted away to a sultry afternoon in a Tuscan villa, sprawled across an old, gold Florentine four-poster, the breeze from the open window caressing my sun-drenched skin as he burrowed deep between my tawny thighs and absorbed the very soul of me...

Back in Sloane Square, I stuck my chest out, pulled my stomach in, raised myself up to my full height (5'3"), combed my fingers through my wind-blown hair and sashayed up to him.

'Josh?' I enquired hopefully, a trace of moistness spreading across the gusset of my black lace thong. I tilted my head expectantly to one side, smiling my most seductive smile.

'*Noh*,' he replied with a foreign accent, and looked straight past me to greet another young hunk emerging from the station. Well at least I'd got one thing right – he was Italian!

As I turned away, my sails slightly less billowy than before, my eyes lit upon a short, plump, rusty-haired boy in a navy anorak who I knew with absolute certainty to be Josh. I thought for a millisecond about heading home, but that would have been cruel and unkind. Sighing in resignation, I approached him with a maternal smile and introduced myself.

Josh looked like he'd just been told he was next in line to the throne. His eyes darted wildly this way and that as if searching for an escape route. Close up he looked about twelve and I wasn't sure if he'd even started shaving. He took one step forward, two steps back, then opened and closed his mouth like a gasping goldfish. I wasn't sure whether to grab a towel or call the emergency services. He was either about to pass out or piss himself.

'Shall we have that coffee?' I suggested. Or are you just going to stand there all day gawping? I walked towards Oriel with him in hot pursuit panting like a puppy. We went downstairs and I settled myself into one of the big, comfy leather armchairs.

'Ca - ca- ca...' he said.

'Yes please. Decaf, ' I answered presuming he was offering me a ca-ca-cappuccino and not telling me he'd just bricked himself. Josh stuttered to the bar and rattled the two cups back to the table. I went into idle chatter mode to put him at his ease, commenting on the traffic, the weather and had he been waiting long? He answered as best he could, but kept blinking at me with his mouth slightly open.

I think I was the walking-talking incarnation of his deepest, darkest fantasies. Either that, or he had an affliction.

'So Josh,' I said, breaking a lengthening silence. 'You seem a little less sure now than when we spoke on the phone. What on earth made you answer my ad?'

He blushed to the tips of his wispy, blond lashes and cleared his throat.

'When I was at school,' he began, 'me and my mates all fancied one another's mums...we used to call them "yummy mummies"...we all reckoned we'd like to...you know...' and he laughed a nervous little high-pitched laugh.

'...and did you?' I asked, already knowing the answer.

'Nah,' he answered, his baby face full of regret. 'Don't think they fancied us lot. Load of grubby fifteen-year-olds with dirty fingers and even dirtier minds!'

Poor little bugger, I thought, but still, I admired his balls and his honesty. I decided to have a bit of fun with it – give him a run for his money. I surreptitiously undid the top button of my shirt and leaned forward across the table flashing my cleavage at him.

'And since then?' I asked. 'Any luck? You're not at school any more, are you?' and I ran the tip of my tongue across my upper lip.

Josh's pink face blotched up like a pepperoni pizza.

'I never got a chance...but I'd like to...oh, I would...' and his eyes devoured the dish of juicy breasts I'd set before him.

'And what about girls your own age?' I asked. 'Don't you date any of them?'

'Yea...'course...' he shrugged, his eyes moving rapidly between my mouth and my chest. 'But *they* haven't got what *you've* got...'

'And in an ideal world,' I asked, going for the kill. 'What would *you* like to happen next?'

'I'dliketogotoahotelroomandhavesexwithyou.' Crikey! He was clearly taking *The Graduate* theme very seriously. I had to admire his candour, and I wondered what would happen if I said: 'OK let's go.' In the context of the advert, I guess he thought I was his due.

'Does anyone know you're here?' I asked, softening my tone.

'Yeah, my best mate Alex. He wanted to know if you had a friend.'

This was getting better! I pictured Josh and Alex jerking-off behind the bike sheds as they planned a foursome with Peggy Mitchell and Pat Butcher. I bit my bottom lip to stop from laughing, then leaned back in my chair, inadvertently reneging on the breast deal.

Josh, realising his proposition had fallen on barren ground, flushed a deeper shade of crimson and tried to hide his face in the bottom of his coffee cup. He raised himself slightly off his seat and effected a small adjustment inside his trousers. I felt really mean, but he'd probably grow up to be a bastard anyway so I was punishing him ahead of the crime. (Oooh! that sounded bitter.)

'Do all young men fancy older women then?' I continued, as a point of social research.

'I think so,' Josh replied. 'Maybe we could open an agency? I'll provide the blokes, you bring along your lady friends. We could make a fortune!'

His suggestion of a potentially lucrative commercial opportunity showed some maturity and it actually sounded like quite a good idea. Judging by the response to my ad, there obviously was a gap in the market. However, my immediate agenda did not include 'whorehouse madam' or taking this randy little boy on as a business partner.

'So are we going anywhere with our new friendship then?' he asked, trying to ignite some enthusiasm on my part.

I'm going home, babes. And you're going back to your schoolboy fantasy.

'I've had quite a lot of replies,' I explained gently, 'so I'm going to carry on, er, interviewing. It's been lovely meeting you Josh, and good luck with everything.'

He followed me somewhat dejectedly out onto the street and we shook hands. He did that awkward ducking and diving move again in a failed attempt to kiss me goodbye. I felt sorry as I walked away, like I'd stolen his fantasy and crushed it underfoot.

As I reached my car he texted me: I want to see you again. Let me know you get home safely.

I muttered 'lamb' under my breath, dismissed him from my thoughts and wondered if the real deal was ever going to come my way.

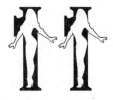

KEITH

THE TEASER GEEZER

During the first influx of calls, one of the guys who'd piqued my interest was a 29-year-old Essex boy called Keith (or 'Keef' as he introduced 'imself). Not my type at all, but needs must when the devil drives (a white van). Keef was definitely a geezer. The minute I heard his voice I thought 'bit o' rough', which was attractive in a 'Lady and the Tramp' sort of way. He left me an articulate and informative message outlining his lifestyle and social aspirations, all delivered in an estuary accent, which is a bit of an oxymoron – rather like the term 'happy marriage' or 'considerate builder' which was, in fact, what he was. I think they call them Water Duct & Pipe Fitting Operatives these days – plumber to you and me. How useful, I thought – if he can't sort out some of my pipes, he can sort out the others and I put him on my list of definite maybes. After the non-starters I'd met so far, I decided to give him a call.

Surprisingly, we got on rather well and had a flirtatious and rather intimate conversation during which the lady in me allowed herself to be titillated by the tramp in him. I found him quite intriguing. Despite having left school at fifteen with no qualifications, he came across as well-read and quick-witted. I had to remind myself not to be such a crashing snob or to judge people by their accents. Frankly, if I had the choice, I'd rather date Alfie Moon than Brian Sewell. Unsure in which category to place him, I told Keef I was going to 'put him behind my ear for later' and we ended the conversation on a high note exchanging email addresses and promising to continue what we'd started. And so began a cyber affair which grew ever more erotic as the days went by.

Keef had a fertile imagination and a lyrical delivery which totally belied his rougher roots. Here are some excerpts from our early correspondence:

Dear Mrs Robinson...Wendy...if I may?
Many thanks for phoning back, it was nice to hear from you and I'm not at all surprised you've been busy with replies! It was a delight to see your enticing, subtle, yet provocative advert. So much so that my long-standing, discerning appreciation, lust and desire for the most elegant, stylish, sophisticated, slender, accomplished older woman could not be ignored.
Attached is my photo, taken a couple of years ago, I've not changed...just lost the sun-baked look. I'm usually the other side of a camera but please let me know what you think, and if you like the look of me perhaps you could send your photo by return? My sensual, erotic imagination runs wild

at the thought of mixing business with pleasure...
does yours?
Yours in anticipation
Keith x

He sent me a photo of himself on holiday with his girlfriend
with a black strip across her eyes to protect her anonymity.
Very thoughtful, don't you think, considering he was
currently searching for sex elsewhere! He was still with
this girl and had told me on the phone that they were
about to move in together to try for a baby! That should
have stopped me in my tracks but there was still something
about him that fascinated me. Facially he looked quite
ordinaire, the sort of chap you see heading through the
turnstile at a football match or playing pool down the pub.
Nice bod though – very fit – and so I replied:

Hi Keith,
You're quite the wordsmith, aren't you? You certainly
have a comprehensive vocabulary although I'm
not sure at this early stage I appreciate your mind
running wild...though of course, I can't stop that,
can I? You have definitely let me know what you
expect. I prefer to take things slowly and see what
pans out. Starting with low expectations often leads
to delightful surprises. I know the Mrs Robinson/
Benjamin connotation is a metaphor for swift
seduction, but that is not what I'm about. Hope
you are not disappointed! I'm not saying it may
not happen at some point, but it would be wrong to
presume it's a fait accompli. Thanks for your photo.
It's hard to tell chemistry from a picture, although
I am very intuitive and I normally know in the first
second if there is any. I'm not sure in this case, but

I am willing to find out! As requested, I attach a recent pic of myself.

The following day he wrote back:

Dear Wendy,
Thanks for your compliments. I totally agree about having realistic expectations... I've often built an ideal up in my mind, only to be disappointed when things didn't turn out as I expected. Your way is much better...but patience is required on the part of the eager young man! If the chemistry exists, the slow, seductive path could lead to wonderful times. Many thanks for your photo, you are a very attractive woman...and I'd love to find out more about you, particularly what you'd ideally like to achieve by placing such a personal ad...you must have a fantasy situation to tell? I'd like to speak with you again before too long, but I'd rather not call the number in the paper. If you'd like to chat please tell me when you might call, so as not to catch me at work or in company...or do you have a number I could call you? If, however, you'd prefer to correspond for a while, I don't mind at all. Hope to hear from you soon.
Yours
Keith x

This *dénouement* continued for a week or so but I soon decided to crank it up a notch and meet Keef face to face. Although I was enjoying the flirtatious exchange, dangling the carrot of my affections just out of his reach was proving as frustrating for me as it was for him.

We arranged our rendezvous for 6 p.m. at The Elgin opposite Maida Vale station, which is my local wine bar. Having had a couple of wasted journeys, I wasn't prepared to displace myself yet again for another bloke who was probably not The One. I arrived on time, shortly before Keef, who looked clean and tidy, dressed in black jeans, a white t-shirt, a black leather jacket and shiny black shoes, with his hair individually spiked in a Gareth Gates from *Pop Idol* kind of way. He wasn't really my type, but he was charming and well-mannered and clearly rather taken with me.

'You're even better looking than your photo,' he sch-moozed as he handed me my drink, and as the evening wore on, I found being in a public place with such an attentive and appreciative young man quite a turn-on. Keef was comfortable in his skin and confident of his own masculinity – another attractive trait. He spoke about his home life, but only because I asked, and entertained me with stories of women in whose houses he had worked. The desperate housewife is still trying to seduce tradesmen in the most banal of ways: walking into the bathroom in her lingerie when she knows damn well he's in there, flashing too much cleavage as she bends to put his tea down, ask-ing if he wouldn't mind zipping up her dress. He told the tales with an engaging twinkle in his eye and an hour or so later, having necked two rather large Bloody Marys, I could easily have become one of those women and toppled over backwards with my legs in the air.

After a couple of hours of close togetherness, Keef apologised and said he had to go. I was rather disappointed but the bond had been established and sexual anticipation was in the air as we walked out into the street. Keef immediately put his arm around my waist and drew me towards him for a kiss goodnight. As we lingered cheek to cheek, I breathed in his pheromone scent and felt my nipples tingle. He was horny and now so was I. We agreed to keep in touch and I drove home on a high, warmed by the promise of future ecstasy with this hot, young stud. A couple of hours later, this email came through:

Dear Wendy

Although I feel bad, dishonest and somewhat guilty about my current situation with my girlfriend, I also feel compelled in many ways to build on what we may have started tonight. I just wished I could have met you when I was much younger... You could have had yourself a 17-year-old after all! I am very attracted to you, both mentally and physically. I loved your mannerisms, your eyes, hair and lips...your laugh, your painted nails and, from what I could tell, your wonderful, delicate, petite figure. I found your posture...the way that you sat and arched your back during conversation, very appealing and quite flirtatious whether you were conscious of it or not...it exaggerated your form...which I most certainly admired. When we parted, I enjoyed kissing you on both cheeks. I loved the slight touch of your waist and would have adored an embrace... You're my sort of woman Wendy!...I guess you could say that I'm quite tuned in with my sensual, feminine and erotic side... For me, this is dangerous ground...but I want to go further, one step at a time, even if nothing (serious) ever happened between us... I just love the idea of it... I can almost taste the excitement... but, like you said...we'll see what unfolds. So Wendy, you know how I feel about you...I'd like to know what you think and feel about me...please

be as honest, frank and as free with your words as you know how.
Regards
Keith x

Hi Keith,
I cannot say you have not been in my thoughts today...and whatever I feel, I feel in a good way! I really liked your look, although if asked to specify, it would be hard to say why! I could see you had taken trouble with your appearance – freshly-shaved, hair well gelled, smart clothes, good shoes – all important to me. I like the thought of you getting ready to meet me, deciding what to wear etc. – again an exploration of your egoist/feminine side. Getting ready for a date is such a girly thing, but this is no aspersion on your very obvious masculinity! Your eloquence and insightful dissection of the situation impresses me – it seems out of context with who you appear to be, given that you have been working since age 16, with little or no Higher Education. Just goes to show the University of Life is the best a guy can get! You have an intuitive and perceptive mind and I like that too.

Thanks for all your compliments about my appearance and persona. I confess to not having been aware of 'arching my back' and I was not trying to be overtly provocative. Of course when a woman is attracted to a man, all sorts of subliminal body language kicks in.

Your domestic situation is your problem. I will not make it mine. It's up to you to decide how you want to deal with it, only bear in mind that whatever we may become to each other, it is unlikely to last or be much more than a delightful interlude. Your life path has far to travel whereas I am well down the road of mine. I am cynical, yes, but also realistic and stopped being an idealist long ago... Hedonism is the name of the game, grab it where you can!

So what now, sweetie? I cannot quite work out from your daily agenda what sort of time you have available. Personally, as mentioned, I prefer a slow build-up – lighting scented candles, preparing drinks, a delicious meal, listening to music by the fire, exploring thoughts and feelings – and none of this can be done in a rush during the afternoon. I don't know if you have to report back or if you are able to disappear from time to time...

Those brief seconds standing by my car were quite powerful...I felt the electricity pass between us and your touch fired something up. I would like to enjoy more of that...and for longer...and of course you can call me anytime...

Wendy xx

To which he replied:

Dear Wendy,
What a relief... I showed you my cards and you didn't shoot me down in flames!... Jokes aside, I'm very happy to have met you last night, I'm glad we enjoyed each other's company and I'm delighted... aroused and quite chuffed that we find ourselves equally attracted to one another. Sometimes the imbalance in attraction makes for difficult progress but it looks like we could enjoy some

very intimate, warm, tender, sensual and hopefully erotic... adventurous... and open-minded fun... (I should stop there before I get carried away.) Likewise Wendy, many thanks for your comments and compliments... I appreciate your sincerity very much. I try to make the best of what I've got even if I don't have the time or the funds to be shopping for the latest styles. Like you, I also love the thought of my date getting ready to go out... I am a self-confessed admirer of slender, elegant ladies whose penchants for beautiful, overpriced lingerie and vast collections of footwear know no bounds! As mentioned, I have, over the years, had quite a few lady clients with sumptuous homes and wardrobes to match. As a young man I found it such an arousing hardship...especially when one fancied the client so much that one blushed each time she came into the room with tea, for a chat...and to tease. I learnt quite a lot about those women from the clothes they bought and often saw their taste in lingerie lying around their bathrooms.

Morning, lunchtime or afternoon meetings are all legitimate. I could meet you after work some evenings (if you liked the idea of a tradesman arriving at your door...to measure you up of course) for a couple of hours or for most of the night. I cherish the thought of afternoon sex... fantastic, frantic and erotic...becoming aroused with each other... provocative behaviour, slow seduction...sensual, insatiable, blissful...hard, fast and tender times. There's too much to write, too many comments and suggestions to make. Email is good but conversation is much nicer. I too felt something exciting last night as we parted... I'd love to

meet you one afternoon, when I would adore
an embrace...a touch, a kiss and to feel your
sensuality...but then to leave before the slow build-
up became the shortest seduction in history! If this
appeals to you...just drop me a short reply.
I could call you tomorrow, about 6pm?
Yours...
Keith x

We arranged to meet again, this time at my home, in
the late afternoon of the following week. I'd had a stressful
day, and was suffering with a lingering headache and didn't
really feel in the mood, but I was loath to cancel as I thought
the r 'n r would do me good. Keith arrived straight from work
and the first thing that struck me was the animal smell of
unwashed male. Although it was getting chilly, I suggested
a walk in the park opposite, thinking this might help
clear my head and the air. As we walked, we talked
about everything and nothing, a totally un-erotic
conversation between two complete strangers trying to re-
fertilise the common ground they'd begun planting in cyber
space.

He spoke a lot about his failing relationship with his
girlfriend in which I had no interest whatsoever. Hearing
him talk about his domestic problems acted like a bucket of
ice on any ardour I may have been harbouring. The daytime
meeting was far too sober. I needed the night and some
alcoholic stimulant to get me going. We returned to my flat
where Keith's powerful pheromones were making my head
worse. I didn't want to offend him by suggesting he take a
shower as he may have thought this was a preamble to sex
which actually was the last thing on my mind.

I gave him a beer and poured myself a Scotch and ginger
and we sat at opposite ends of the sofa struggling to make

conversation: another classic case of reality killing fantasy. We'd expressed ourselves so freely in writing, but face to face we were virtually tongue-tied. And then, abruptly, my headache started to hammer and I just wanted him gone. I pressed my finger to my right temple and frowned deeply.

'I'm sorry, Keith,' I said. 'I'm really not feeling that great...' which sounded like the classic excuse much beloved of women who need to extricate themselves from tricky situations. He looked utterly dejected, especially when I stood up to make it clear the date was over.

He gathered his belongings and left self-consciously with his tail between his legs. As I closed the door, I felt quite disappointed that the build-up and mental foreplay had all but fizzled out with no tangible result. I made myself a cup of hot, sweet tea and took a couple of pills.

Later that evening, just before bed, I checked my emails.

Dear Wendy,
I felt a little awkward when I left you this evening not knowing what you were thinking...you seemed preoccupied and a little twitchy... My departure was quite abrupt and slightly off key...and I don't know how you felt at the time? Although I acted tonight (correct me if I'm wrong) as if I had no inclination to pounce on you whatsoever (I didn't want to take advantage or ruin your invitation to join you for a drink)...I was, in fact, seducing you in my thoughts. Your body language was less flirtatious than the first time we met...therefore I didn't make any presumptions. Our conversation was interesting, pleasant and enjoyable but not

intimate or provocatively enchanting...although I would have begun on that subject had you not hinted that I should leave! What I might ideally be seeking by meeting you is respectful, discreet, intimate, mutually rewarding, passionate, ravishing, unbridled morning or afternoon sex...once a week...twice a week...once a fortnight...whatever we wanted. I love your looks, your figure and I love the thought of giving your body and mind ultimate pleasure...and in turn, receiving mine... Frankly Wendy, it appears that we are both intelligent and highly sexed, yet discerning people...and if you're even just slightly attracted to me and the thought of exploring your most intimate, erotic, sensual desires...then I propose we should meet again, but swap the pleasant chit-chat for open-minded, honest, sexy conversation and behaviour...to kiss, to touch...something I feel we both want but are equally unsure about...right or wrong? (Perhaps right for you but with someone else!) Could you live with the idea of having me as your 'bit on the side', not you as mine... You could use me when you want to, to have me touch, kiss, lick, tongue and taste you...if that's all you wished for...have me massage you, make love to you tenderly and bathe you...or simply fuck you...hard and fast...quickly or for hours...as your mood dictated....??? I miss the feeling of being totally, sexually submerged with a beautiful woman and giving all that I have to give...the chance to have you would be a fine thing.

With kind regards

Keith

By the time I finished reading this, I'd gone off the whole idea of him. The fact that he only offered me morning or afternoon sex really bugged me. These were not the times that suited me and besides, *I* wanted to call the shots. Although I wasn't looking for any kind of commitment, a man who had to be home for supper was as good as married, and that was not what I had in mind when I placed the ad.

Although I had some regard and respect for him, I didn't really fancy him sober as much as I had when I'd been pissed. Unsure how to let him down gently, I wrote this rather dismissive note hoping he would get the message.

Keith
Without rambling on in too much detail, it seems that you are free for sex mornings or afternoons, neither of which times are convenient for me!! I know that is very simplified but I also know I want more than that: a lover to suit my agenda not mine to suit his. Also you are clearly committed to your relationship, and in that context you had no business answering my ad! Devote yourself to your own life and find the sexual addition you seek elsewhere, perhaps closer to home.
Sorry to be so blunt, but for me, although there is some chemistry between us, the aforesaid complications would cloud the issue. You already have baggage and will have a lot more in the future if your baby plans bear fruit...
If at some later date, I can find a role for you in my life, I will certainly let you know...thanks for an amusing interlude and I hope all your dreams come true.
W

That temporarily put the lid on Keith. Needless to say, perversity being a feminine trait, I found I quite missed the repartee. I went out for a drink with Ozzie, the naval officer, but he was far too proper and correct. I also met a young, but instantly forgettable Mancunian called Rod. About ten days later, and I can't say I wasn't pleased, I heard from Keith again:

Hi Wendy,

In your last email you talked of finding a 'role' for me. Keeping on that theme, if you favour good continuity and would enjoy playing the tease some more, I'd love to be kept up-to-date with your success with the ad... I sit on the casting couch each day waiting, wishing for a career break from my sitcom relationship. A role for me to play for you...which I would hope would not be a 'bit part'...perhaps not the leading man either, but behind the scenes...if you see what I mean!! I'm good with my tools and know a bit about props, lighting, cameras and action...!!! Seriously though, as a sexually liberated, open-minded, worldly woman, have you ever been persuaded by a past lover to pose for discreet, sensual, erotic, 'only teasing' photos? Hope you don't mind me asking. I've been on both sides of the camera... the feelings and results were wonderful. You would be a stunning subject. Some attractive mature women have more visual appeal and style than younger 'obviously' beautiful women. Until we hopefully meet again, I shall remain happily tucked behind your ear. I would love to take you out for a meal, dinner or lunch, and see how life is treating you, if you'd be pleased to accept?

My best wishes and love
Keith x

During the course of one of our conversations, he had mentioned this great love and hobby of his: photography. When he asked if I would be willing to model for him, I laughed if off, but took the suggestion as a compliment. When I told a girlfriend about it, however, she was horrified.

'Are you completely mad?' she demanded. 'You'll end up on the internet!'

I hadn't thought of that! I believed Keith to be honourable but my girlfriend said I was being naive. This wound me up so I replied rather arrogantly:

Hi Keith
Since you have, yet again, written so eloquently, it would be impolite not to reply! I must point out that I have had several offers from men to do exactly what you are suggesting, and I can assure you more get turned down than get accepted.
Yes, of course, it is very flattering and a million women out there would just drool at the thought, and grab the offer by the balls, so to speak! I have not cut off from you entirely...I just haven't really decided what I want to do and you may have to wait a while for me to make up my mind... In the meantime, live your life and be patient...you never know...your day may come...
W

The next day, there he was again, trying to prise open my (in)box.

Hi W,

I have been thinking constantly on the topic of sensual, erotic photography and I want to pursue this pent-up interest with passion. If you're seriously interested and not just teasing me...as you do so often (which I do enjoy by the way)... I'd love to arrange an evening to meet you and share our ideas to see what kind of images you'd like to create.

I seem to have inherited a sense of taste and mild perversion and it's too strong to ignore...and you Wendy, are an ideal model...with I imagine, an excellent collection of beautiful lingerie and elegant attire to make good use of?

Do let me know how you feel about this...

Love Keith XX

It's a reflection on how empty my life must have been at that time that I actually considered this offer and so again, I replied:

Hi Keith,

I will be honest: I am drawn to the idea in principle but with a multitude of reservations. Firstly, the absolute and irrevocable understanding that the images must remain MY property and not for any type of distribution! My sense of eroticism tempts me because I know a 'soft porn' photo shoot would create a tantalising, egocentric encounter...with only one inevitable conclusion. However, I can only imagine doing it in very muted light and that probably would not be sufficient for the photography!

Also, I am very susceptible to sounds, smells and

atmospheres and I would need to be in exactly the right mood, with the right music, incense, candles and other accoutrements to unleash my inhibitions enough for this event to take place. At this moment, my acceptance seems unlikely but thank you for asking.

Love

W xx

P.S. I feel it only fair to tell you that I have had a very interesting reply to my ad: a young man I like very much who is happily <u>unencumbered</u>. I may be off the radar while I see how it goes.

The P.S. was fabrication, a way of getting Keith off my case, but as some savant once said:

'Be careful what you wish for...'

BEN

THE CLOSEST THING TO CRAZY...

Just as I was beginning to despair that this whole Mrs Robinson thing was a complete waste of time, I got a new voicemail from a guy called Ben. The moment he began to speak I knew that, at last, I'd found my Benjamin. I'd done nothing but press the delete button on the last several messages, sometimes not even letting them get further than the words: 'Er...my name's...'. It's amazing how judgemental one can become and I'd learnt to judge fast. If the voice didn't fit, my instinct told me nothing else would.

As I listened to Ben, I became more and more enraptured. Ben made all my bells peal at once; Ben sounded just young enough to teach and just old enough to learn; Ben had a voice so mellifluous, I imagined him gargling with honey.

'I must confess to a terrible weakness for attractive, older women...' he purred – and like the girl in *Jerry Maguire*, he had me at 'Hallo'.

I called him back immediately.

'Are you available to talk to Mrs Robinson?' I enquired, assuming the role of wanton temptress. He responded with a throaty chuckle that made me want to rake my fingers through his hair and drag him down towards me on the bed. It was instant, heart-stopping, gut-churning, clit-quivering chemistry. We slipped easily into suggestive conversation and a mutual curiosity was rapidly established. Amazing how you can connect with some people straight away yet with others it never happens no matter how hard you try...

In the course of our discussion, I found out that he was 6' tall, with dark hair and blue eyes. What he did for a living was a bit nebulous but he alluded to an address in Fulham and a cottage in the Cotswolds, and mentioned *en passant* a penchant for polo. I had a Jilly Cooper moment as I pictured him galloping across Smith's Lawn on an Arab stallion, his sinewy thigh muscles rippling in their tight jodhpurs, his long leather boots set firm in the stirrups as he swung his mallet...It was all so glorious and manly. I was excited. Very excited.

Neither of us seemed keen to end the conversation (The Rules say you should bring it to a close within ten minutes but bugger them!) and Ben asked if we could meet the following Monday afternoon as he planned to be 'in town'. I said I wasn't sure; I knew I had a business appointment, but had already decided to change it. We said goodbye in clear expectation of an ongoing rapport and my instinct put its arms around me and gave me a hug.

I hovered through the next day with such a grin on my face, I'm surprised someone didn't smack me. Ben had bounced me right back up where I wanted to be and my already inflated ego was rocketing to ever dizzier heights. I duly rearranged my Monday meeting and spent the entire weekend lying prone across the playing fields of fantasy land.

♀

First thing on Monday morning, I texted him. I `can make it this afternoon after all. How about you?`

`Yes. Brilliant. Where and When?` came the eager reply. I punched the air with a victorious YES!!

We arranged to meet at 5 p.m. on the corner of Bond Street and Brook Street just outside Fenwicks fashion store. Because of Ben's obvious *savoir faire*, I felt it my duty to dress the part. I selected a black crepe skirt with a Chanel-style (Zara actually!) cream and black top. I put on a new pair of Barely Black glossy tights and my high-heeled, black suede court shoes. After trying various hairstyles ranging from Catherine Deneuve to Cyndi Lauper, I tied my hair back in a velvet scrunchie with a couple of tendrils framing my face. I completed the outfit with one of my most treasured accessories, a real black quilted Chanel handbag.

Feeling confident that Ben was about to rock my world, I drove into town, parked my car and walked along Bond Street to the appointed meeting place. I was running a few minutes early and as the time drew near, my confidence dissolved into nervous apprehension. What the hell did I think I was doing waiting for strange, young men on street corners?

I stood outside Fenwicks looking left and right. A few minutes and many people passed, and my earlier bravado totally evaporated as self-doubt and embarrassment took hold of me. What would my mother say if she knew? And my children?! I paced up and down trying to spot him before he spotted me, certain that everyone who walked by knew exactly what I was up to and was mocking me behind my back. I then realised I'd broken my 'Must Exchange Photos' rule yet again and despite his magnetic charm on the telephone, it occurred to me that Ben might actually look like the bastard child of Bilbo Baggins and Tugboat Annie.

I went back into the store a couple of times and wandered blindly through the jewellery department trying to pass the time and realign my chakras. My stomach was churning like a concrete mixer and an attack of wind seemed imminent. At 5.10 p.m. I went back outside but he still wasn't there. I decided to give him until 5.15 (and then extend that to 5.30).

At 5.12 p.m. a tall, elegant, composed young man came striding along Bond Street towards me with a look of hopeful expectation in his eyes. If he was thinking: please let it be her, I was thinking: PLEASE let it be him. He was dressed in a cavalry-twill overcoat with a brown velvet collar, over a charcoal-grey pin-striped three-piece suit. He passed my shoe test straight away: very grown-up, highly-polished, black lace-up brogues. As he strode towards me, he swung a slightly-battered pigskin briefcase. My first impression was that he was out of his time; he looked like a 1930s character from an Evelyn Waugh story. A bright young thing, a 'Vile Body', my very own Art Deco boy. Gosh! I thought, adjusting my language to suit the period. How spiffing! He stopped at my side.

'He-llo-w!' he murmured conspiratorially. He leaned forward to peck my cheek, and intimacy oozed from his every pore. And as I looked up admiringly into his bright blue eyes, I knew that in the not too distant future we were unquestionably going to have sex.

♀

Ben was not conventionally handsome, but possessed of such old-fashioned charm that I was instantly enthralled.

'Shall we?' he proposed, gently guiding my elbow as he motioned me to cross the road. Keeping a respectful distance, we walked to the Balls Brothers wine bar on the corner of South Molton Street and descended the wooden staircase to the subtly-lit cellar. It was empty but for a barman polishing glasses. We went through to a little private room at the back and Ben asked me what I would like to drink.

'White wine, please,' I answered, plumming my voice up slightly to match his.

I watched him with fascination as he walked to the bar. He looked exactly as he'd sounded on the phone: aristocratic, self-assured, possibly even landed gentry. He had very thick, dark, curly hair, an angular nose, a strong jaw weakening slightly towards the chin, high cheekbones and a full mouth the colour of raspberries. His skin was pale, almost translucent, and from what I could see, his body formed a perfect triangle: broad shoulders tapering down to exceedingly slim hips. I felt rather breathless and fluttery.

Ben's briefcase rested where he'd left it on the chair opposite. I peered at the monogram. It didn't match his initials. Or he'd lied about his name.

He returned to the table and placed the wine glasses down, then sat on the bentwood chair with his long legs widely parted. He shot his cuffs and I noticed a glint of gold at his wrists. My eyes darted down to his crotch and back up again. We raised our drinks in a toast to each other and I took a long sip. Only being a social drinker, and on an empty stomach, I get tipsy very quickly and by the time I was half way through my first glass, I was full of flights of fancy. Ben would have had no problem tempting me into a hotel room. Mrs Robinson was alive and well and tippling in Mayfair.

'So tell me,' I questioned, seeking refuge in familiar territory, 'what made you answer the ad?'

'I've had some form with older women' he drawled as if he'd backed a couple who'd come first and second in the Cheltenham Gold Cup. 'One in particular... They seem to...er...*happen* to me...' and he raised an eyebrow and smiled.

'Do tell?' I enquired, leaning forward with my chin on my hand.

'A neighbour of ours...friend of the family...' he hesitated. 'Er...I was about 20. Still a virgin actually...' and his eyes grew slightly misty at the memory. 'Her husband was often abroad on business and she would drop round, usually when my parents were out. She said she was lonely...felt abandoned...and one thing led to another. I think I consoled her rather well...and she taught me...' he smiled knowingly '...a trick or two...'

'Did your parents ever find out?'

'Good grief no! They'd have deported me to the French Foreign Legion! The woman's marriage broke up soon after – I may have had something to do with that... They sold the farm and she moved away but it gave me a taste for...how shall I put this?... A riper kind of fruit?' and he winked and raised his glass in salute.

'At thirty-three, with the sort of life you lead – all those town and country pursuits – don't you get introduced to a lot of young...er...fillies?'

He shrugged and chuckled again. God, he was sexy.

'Mmmmm, of course I do, but they just don't attract me. The last one I met – well let's just say I was rather more drawn to her mother. Those girls are superficial, only interested in marriage and babies – such hard work. An older woman, now she knows *exactly* what she wants...'

I nodded. What an astute young man. On performance so far: full marks!

'Would you like another drink?' Ben asked politely noticing my almost empty glass.

'Only if you'll join me,' I answered reaching into my handbag for my purse.

'No, please...' he insisted leaning forward to stay my hand. I glanced up at him and our eyes caught and held for a long moment. Ben's eyes narrowed as if he was remembering something then he peeled himself away and returned to the bar. A few more people had wandered in but we still had the little back room to ourselves. I took out my compact and checked myself in the mirror. Nothing smudged or dislodged. No spinach between my teeth. A little flushed though, but that was to be expected.

Ben returned with the drinks and we carried on talking about work, travel, life and love. I tend to skirt over my past relationships: too many marriages, divorces and affairs, and too many years to add up if they care to do the maths. I prefer to release information on a need-to-know basis, just dotting my conversation with dateless entertaining anecdotes. Business-wise, Ben seemed to have his finger in a lot of pies but didn't reveal the details of any of them. I tried to find out more by commenting on the monogram on his briefcase, but he said he'd inherited it from an uncle, which seemed plausible enough. It was ancient and rather battered and I felt guilty for having doubted him.

Just before 6.30 p.m. Ben looked at his watch.

'I'd love to prolong this, Tiger' (Ooah! How cool was

that!) 'but I've got a train to catch. Staying overnight in Oxford. Meeting in the morning. I should get back...'

I nodded regretfully and we both stood up. He helped me on with my jacket and donned his coat. We walked up the stairs and out onto the street. Ben looked around, then stuck his arm out to hail a taxi.

'Are you going to Paddington?' I asked impulsively. 'We can share it, if you don't mind. It's on my way home,' Despite my nearby car, I was in no fit state to drive.

'Wonderful,' he smiled and held the door open for me to climb in.

As soon as we'd sat down and the cab took off, Ben took my hand and clutched it tightly in his. He turned towards me and stared very tenderly into my eyes. My heart tripped as I looked back at him then lowered my gaze. Ben placed one finger under my chin, raised my face up to his and kissed me softly on the mouth. It was a chaste though lingering kiss and the touch of his lips melted me. God... Should I invite him home? No. I must get a grip. It would be too much, too soon. It would ruin everything. He'd have to wait. *I'd* have to wait. I knew I would see him again and the build-up would be tantalising.

The journey to Paddington was all too short and soon the cab pulled up, its engine chugging. Ben reached for his wallet.

'Don't worry' I said touching his arm. 'I'll get this.'

'Thanks,' he said and leaned towards my ear. 'I'll...er...see you very soon?'

'WHEN???' I wanted to scream but I nodded keenly and looked longingly at him. He squeezed my hand. And then he was gone.

Later that evening on the bus back into town to collect my car, I texted him: Lovely to meet you...see you again soon I hope xx and instantly regretted it.

Always let them do the chasing – I should know that well enough. He didn't reply which only compounded my self-reproach. Now I had to play my least favourite sport: the waiting game.

BEN AGAIN

After a rather impassioned start, Ben annoyingly went off the radar. I had a suspicion he may have worked for MI5, so vague had he been about what he actually did. A couple of weeks went past without a word which was most frustrating, and then quite unexpectedly at 11 a.m. one Monday morning, while I was at my desk doing some work, my mobile phone rang and a withheld number came up on the screen. Certain it was either Kitchens Direct or some over-enthusiastic American shouting 'Con-gra-chu-lay-tions! You've just won a harliday in Flarida!' I answered rather curtly. My impatience turned to surprise and then softened into pleasure when a half-forgotten voice purred:

'He-ll-ow...is that Mrs R?'

'Who's calling?' I asked, determined to give him a hard time for having left it so long. My question was answered with the unmistakeable throaty chuckle.

'Oh!' I said, softening my tone. 'It's you. Well, well...to

what do I owe the pleasure?'

'The pleasure is all mine,' he replied in debonair fashion. 'And a long-delayed pleasure it is too. I've been rather busy. New project. Had to do a bit of travelling. Brussels... Munich...that sort of thing. But how are *you?*'

We soon picked up the connection and slid back into sexy-speak.

'Are you by any chance free on Thursday evening?' Ben asked, finally getting to the point of his call. 'I'm coming up to London for a business meeting, and then...' he paused for effect '...I have a lunch in town on the Friday...'

The implication was not lost on me. He had to stay in London overnight.

'Let me just check my diary,' I answered, knowing full well that even if Scorsese wanted to audition me for a starring role opposite Clooney, he was about to get dumped.

'Thursday's fine,' I confirmed. '...er...anything particular in mind? How about I cook you dinner?'

'What a superb idea!' he enthused. 'But how about *I* cook *you* dinner? I have a way with venison. Or would you prefer pheasant? There's a brace hanging in the barn. Shot 'em last Sunday.'

Being a gastro townie neither of these two gamey suggestions appealed to me. My mind was on a different game altogether. However, the idea of him pottering about in my kitchen wearing nothing but a pinny and a silk cravat conjured up a picture Gordon Ramsay could only aspire to.

'Either would be delicious.' I replied. 'Surprise me. I'll do the starter and the pud.'

'...and I've got a rather good Côtes de Beaune in the cellar. Shall we say around seven o'clock?'

'Perfect. I'll be here. Ready and able.'

'Willing too, I hope?'

It was my turn to answer with a throaty chuckle.

'That, young Benjamin, is for *me* to know and for *you* to find out.'

I hung up the phone and fell across my laptop in a theatrical swoon.

♀

On the Thursday afternoon, I stopped work early and continued what I had begun: the lengthy process of Getting Ready, something which often took days but was designed to look like I'd been born that way.

Oscar Wilde said: 'Sausages and women: if you want to enjoy the experience, never watch the preparation of either' – and how right he was. Depilated like a high-class whore, exfoliated to the deepest layer of my epidermis and moisturised to a level of softness only felt on the bottom cheeks of a new-born baby, I dressed carefully, approving the end result in my full-length bedroom mirror: a black gored skirt which swished as I walked, a cream lace button-through blouse for ease of access and very, very high heels.

I had decided to serve dinner formally in the dining room, instead of my usual place of entertainment: the kitchen. Ben deserved it. It wasn't a snack. It was a *dîner à deux*. I arranged my white hand-embroidered Madeira organdie place mats onto the polished walnut surface of my Art Deco dining-table and set the crystal wine goblets and silver cutlery upon them, neatly aligning everything in perfect symmetry. This was like foreplay to me. Clusters of scented candles were dotted strategically around the room, and it looked magically romantic if not a little contrived.

At seven on the dot, I placed my Dr. Hook Love Songs CD in the player and forwarded the disc to my favourite track. I poured myself a Scotch and ginger and aimed the CD remote.

> *'When your body's had enough of me and I'm lying flat out on the floor*
> *When you think I've loved you all I can, I'm gonna love you a little bit more.'*

I stood there swaying to the music, cradling the ice cold tumbler against my chest. This particular lyric always caused a lurch of longing in my heart and a rush of desire to my loins.

I looked at my watch and went back to the mirror for the umpteenth time to check my make-up. This was the moment before the party starts, when everything's ready but the guests have yet to arrive. You're anxious but excited and you really want the doorbell to ring. I hadn't really thought beyond that point – it was just a moment suspended in time when the world holds its breath and all things are possible.

I was just thinking of applying a little extra blusher when the buzzer made me jump. A natural flush spread across my cheeks like spilt rosé on a cream tablecloth. I rushed to the video entry phone and checked the screen, then breathed deeply to compose myself before picking up the receiver.

'Hello...' I greeted with warmest welcome in my voice. 'All the way to the top, I'm afraid.'

I dimmed the lights, fluffed up my hair one last time, cleared my nervous throat and opened the door just as Ben was climbing the last flight of stairs which led to my door.

'I call it the Robinson workout,' I laughed apologetically. 'You should try it with four carrier bags from Waitrose!'

and I held the door wide open for him to enter.

'Good evening,' Ben smiled as he walked into my flat. I closed the door firmly behind him. Gotcha, I said to myself.

'Let me take your coat,' I offered and removed a good wooden hanger from the hall cupboard.

Ben put his briefcase down and gave me his coat. I hung it up. He adjusted his shirt cuffs beneath his suit jacket and I caught the familiar glimpse of gold at his wrists. I took hold of his arm and pulled it towards me for a closer look. Foxes' heads. Very PC! Very Countryside Alliance.

'May I?' he asked and bent forward to kiss me chivalrously on both cheeks. The subtle scent of aftershave blended with pure essence of male. The aroma entered my blood stream and wound its way through my body igniting little fires in all my erogenous zones. I could have slammed him against the wall and had him fully-dressed right there in the hallway.

'Come through,' I invited instead, and Ben picked up his briefcase and followed me into the kitchen.

I knew he was looking at me as I walked ahead of him and I added a subtle sway to my hips. I did not normally wear a purple satin and black lace basque with suspenders, stockings and cami-knickers beneath my clothes, nor did I ever sport exceptionally high heels around the house; especially not the kind with diamanté ankle straps just begging to be undone by someone's teeth. The little shopping trip for the hidden secrets which I knew, and hoped he would soon find out, made me feel extremely alluring and incredibly sexy. Ben took off his jacket and hung it on the back of a kitchen chair. He undid his cufflinks and rolled up his sleeves revealing pale, slim arms brushed with a down of dark, silky hair. He opened his briefcase and took out a carrier bag which he placed on the work surface. Then he lifted out the bottle of wine and I slid the bottle opener across the counter towards him.

'Would you like to open that now?' I asked. 'Let it breathe a little? I'm having a Scotch and ginger. Shall I make you one?'

'My favourite apéritif!' Ben replied, picking up the corkscrew and inserting it expertly into the bottle top.

'Lots of ice, please' he added, and with the minimum of effort, he uncorked the wine with a satisfying pop.

There is a distinct link between food and foreplay which I'd noted as I'd prepared the creamy vichyssoise earlier that morning. Washing the long, hard, smooth-skinned leeks under the tap, I'd found myself running my hand up and down the firm flesh in a less than culinary manner. I was now thoroughly enjoying being controlled in my own kitchen, Ben playing the role of Super Chef with me as assistant, chopping, grating, stirring and mixing as he prepared the ingredients for the venison marinade. I happily danced attendance upon him, tendering carving knives, wooden spoons and condiments as he required them, intermittently popping cashews and anchovy-stuffed olives into his mouth. As the Scotch warmed and relaxed us both, our movements became quite uninhibited. Every time I fed him, he sucked my fingers while staring at me in a very suggestive way. Although the kitchen was a large eat-in room, we managed to brush past each other at every opportunity as if we were working in a galley on board a very small yacht.

The venison safely in the oven, we proceeded to the dining-table. Ben pulled the chair out for me and once I was seated, he shook out my linen napkin and laid it across my lap. I grinned up at him and he winked back as he wound his sleeves down, replaced his cufflinks and made himself comfortable alongside me. He poured two glasses of wine and raised his in a toast.

'To a very pleasant evening, Mrs Robinson,' he purred and we clinked crystal and drank.

The meal was deliciously lubricated by the fine, fruity wine. The atmosphere between us sparkled with little currents of electricity as each mouthful was digested with pleasure and appreciation. When we had finished our main course, I shooed Ben off to the sofa while I cleared the table. The scented candles flickered, the music played and the fire created a soft, warm glow. It all felt perfect. I carried the tray into the kitchen, loaded the dishwasher, then melted a bar of Green and Black's dark organic chocolate in a bain-marie.

I brought the little bowl into the living-room with a larger bowl of ripe, red strawberries and sat down next to Ben on the sofa. Tilting my head to one side, I glanced up at him through my heavily-mascaraed lashes as I swirled a strawberry around and around in the melted chocolate. With a come-and-get-it look in my eyes, I used the strawberry to lure Ben towards me. He held my gaze and leaned forward then closed his lips around the ripe, red fruit, drawing it into his mouth as he shut his eyes and savoured the chocolate ecstasy. I watched him enjoying the oral sensation.

I picked up and coated another strawberry and popped it between my teeth, leaning provocatively towards Ben. He took the bait, closed the distance between us and bit into the other half. Mouth to mouth, we suckled in unison, giggling as we licked the dripping juices from each other's lips. I felt very young and very happy. He was here, and this was now, and as far as I was concerned, the rest of the world and everything in it could spin away to oblivion.

As our tongues met and a liquid warmth flowed through

me, the sweet flavours of flesh and fruit melded into one. Ben wrapped his arms around me and drew me closer to him. Desire mounted, sizzling through our bodies like a match through touch-paper. From there, the flame just caught and blazed. Ben, panting hard, pulled away briefly, tore off his tie, then re-engaged with my skin in an intoxicating journey from my earlobe to the rise of my cleavage. I arched my back as far as it would comfortably go.

Ben abruptly stopped what he was doing. He pulled away from me on the sofa and ran his hand nervously through his hair. His face was very flushed and he looked anxious, and I was suddenly afraid that he was going to say:

'I'm sorry. I have to go now.'

I blinked at him in fearful expectation, a little frown threatening my brow.

Ben cleared his throat and swallowed nervously. I looked into his eyes for a sign. He sighed, took my hand in his and in the sweetest, most endearing way, he leaned forward and whispered in my ear:

'Dear Mrs Robinson. Is Benjamin allowed to make love to you?'

'Allowed?' I whispered back, relief gushing through me.

'Allowed, you ask?' like Mr Bumble when Oliver asked for more.

'You are *required* to make love to me, Benjamin. I think in the present circumstances it would be churlish not to!' and I brought my hand down to rest lightly on the distended area around his groin.

I raised myself off the sofa, reached out for him and led him down the corridor into my bedroom, made ready earlier with fresh linen and red light bulbs. I paused and turned to him as we reached the side of my bed. I undid my top button and put my arms around his neck. Ben took over, undoing the rest one by one. He peeled off my clothes and let them drop to the floor.

At that moment I knew that if we never went any further, all my efforts had been worthwhile. At twenty-six years his senior, I stood proudly before him: a lady dressed like a whore who felt like a princess.

Ben's eyes glowed with the wonderment of a child on Christmas morning unwrapping a longed-for toy. In almost religious adulation, he sank to his knees, stroking his way down the length of my thighs then back up again. He slid his hands inside the folds of my purple satin cami-knickers. He fondled my buffed and polished cheeks then with one long, slender, probing finger he eased the front of the knickers aside and in a snake-like movement, dived his hot tongue between my rosy labia. Discovering the naked smoothness of my mound, he emitted a shuddering gasp of pleasure and surprise.

'You exquisite *BITCH!*' he exclaimed and began to lap me like a thirsty pussy cat. The agonizing Hollywood waxing had been worth it. His attentions to my most sensitive regions combined with the wicked wantonness of my stance – hips thrust forward, heels as high as a harlot's – rapidly brought on the first of many orgasms that night.

Ben was a cavalier in every sense. He tended me with patience and devotion, worshipping my body with the unselfish experience of a man who truly knows how to please a woman. When he finally mounted me, ours was a wild abandoned ride which reached its zenith time and again yet still sought to travel further. Never had Dr. Hook's lyrics been so appropriate:

When you think I've loved you all I can, I'm going to love you a little bit more...

We collapsed onto the mattress to rest briefly then began again, slower this time teasing each other back to ecstasy, until in the twilight hour between dark and dawn we finally slept spent and sated in each other's arms.

Some time around 6 a.m., I turned over and Ben spooned in close behind me.

'You OK, babe?' I whispered and he peppered my back with little kisses. I sighed very deeply, wishing once again I could preserve this moment forever. I pulled the covers up around us, blanketed in our bliss, and I felt him harden against me, his probing cock nudging between my buttocks. I pushed back into him, raising my leg for ease of access and he slid straight into me. He wrapped his arm around me and fingered my clitoris until our movements quickened to reach yet another mutual climax. As I came down from my euphoria, a deep sense of sadness and loss overwhelmed me. The clock was ticking and the heat of the night was about to surrender to the coldness of day. We slept again until the light woke us.

In an act of déjà vu (same move, different bloke) Ben got up and disappeared into the bathroom to emerge some time later wearing The Robe. I couldn't help but smile. My wish for it to grace as many backs as possible was coming true. He approached the bed and stood over me, smiling down. I smiled back, stretched, reached for the tie-belt and dragged him towards me.

Ben took a step forward close enough for me to stick my hand through the wrap-over and run it up and down his sinewy thigh. My movement came to rest on the up stroke and I probed around inquisitively. His genitalia were neatly arranged and finely formed, and this was the first chance I'd had to appreciate them in their flaccid state. His testicles were plummy, cool and firm as I moulded them in the palm of my hand. His penis felt fleshy and malleable and I couldn't resist rolling the head around between my thumb and forefinger. Ben began tutting in mock reproach as I undid the cord's knot and The Robe fell open. Inclining my head upwards, I took the end of his nice clean penis in my mouth and sucked on it gently. Ben moaned and adjusted his stance as the blood surged through him and hardened his cock yet again.

I crouched up on my hands and knees and took his full erection in my mouth, running my hot tongue up and down the shaft as I gripped the base firmly. I worked steadily and rhythmically until his legs stiffened and his knees began to tremble. As his climax approached, he clutched my head in both his hands leaving me no choice but to receive him as he shot his load into my mouth. I slowed my movements until I was sure he had finished then fell back onto the bed, undecided what to do with my mouthful. It was not, nor ever had been, my 'favourite tipple', despite it allegedly being so good for you. (A PR exercise obviously trumped up by a team of blokes!) It seemed insulting to spit at this point, so I screwed up my eyes and swallowed, a little shudder racking my body as the slimy ejaculate slid down my throat.

Ben shrugged The Robe off and let it fall to the floor. He climbed back onto the bed and straddled me, looking down at my nakedness with lust and admiration. I smiled mischievously up at him then lifted my hips and flashed my hairless pussy at his face. He licked his lips lasciviously, and wriggled down between my legs, taking my bud between his teeth and nibbling on it. Sensations rose rapidly and feeding my fingers through his wet curls, it was my turn to trap his head unforgiving against me, grinding into his face as I reached my goal. The strength of my orgasm astounded me and I spasmed with renewed rapture, unwittingly emitting a sob of gratitude and release. He lapped up my juices one last time then sighing deeply, brought his head to rest contentedly against the inside of my thigh.

Then he looked at his watch, tapped it apologetically and got dressed, ready to leave.

15th Nov. 8.42 a.m.

I can't bear it. Ben's gone and I have no idea when or even IF I'll ever see him again. A deep sense of melancholy and gloom has descended over me and I may just stay in bed for the rest of my life 'cos I simply can't face getting up and going back to the real world. If I stay in my bed – our bed – the bed where we shared such unparalleled joy, I can replay the night over and over and maybe make it real again. God, I wish it was still yesterday and I had it all to look forward to... Now I just feel abandoned and alone. Oh come back, Ben, come back and make me glow again...

A hot tear plopped out of my right eye and landed with a splat onto my diary. I blinked rapidly which released an indulgent flow of loneliness and self-pity.

The remains of Ben's visit are scattered all over the flat and I don't think I shall ever clear them away. It would feel like a desecration of our time together. Last night's washing-up's still in the sink and the bedroom resembles Glastonbury after a fuck fest. I don't remember tying him up or him bonding me, but there's that length of black silk cord from the living-room curtains coiled on the floor like a dead snake and I've no idea how it got there! My heart feels like a lump of lead. I'm drained in mind and body and in grave danger of descending into a black pit of depression and despair...

'I'll call you' he said as he walked out my door.

I'll call you! What the fuck is that supposed to mean??? Why didn't he just kill me before he left? Death by Orgasm. What a way to go...

By the time I got up, showered, dressed and tidied the flat, I felt a little more together. Tired of course, shattered even, but with very good reason. I put Katie Melua on the CD and wailed the words of 'Closest Thing to Crazy' over and over again. As I made the bed (which needed changing, but I didn't want to do that just yet...) I reminded myself how incredibly blessed I was. How many women of my age, or any age, get a night like that to look back on? I phoned my best friend and bored her senseless with the finer details of the past sixteen hours. She listened indulgently and I wondered what life would be like without the blesssed comfort of my girlfriends. As we creak manless into our dotage, we'll have nothing but our memories and each other to rely on.

I locked the night away in my memory bank and got on with my day. I went to bed as early as I could, and as I snuggled down, I reached out and ran my hand along the cool sheet where Ben had lain...then I slumped into a deep sleep filled with unicorns and centaurs galloping across rivers of flowing chocolate.

The following morning, much to my delight, I received this formal hand-written note:

> Dear Tiger,
>   Thank you for a delightful evening... It is wonderful to be able to shut out the rest of the world and spend time with such a lovely girl. I enjoyed every minute of it and will cherish those moments for ever...

What beautiful manners – so courteous and well-bred – a credit to his upbringing and his parents. And the following day, utterly faultless, he called me, leaving me no time at all to obsess, agonise, reproach, become homicidal or suicidal. I almost felt deprived!

After this, Ben kept in fairly regular contact. We established a comfortable pattern and, for the following six months, spent many significant dates together: New Year's Eve, Valentine's Day (and night), Easter weekend and the two Bank Holidays. It was a relationship of sorts. I'd pick him up at Paddington Station and the minute we were home, I'd lock the door to the outside world and we'd disappear into each other. He'd unpack his smart, leather weekend bag, take off his shoes and put on his slippers, and then produce a series of sexy and unusual little gifts for me: a pair of 1950s Christian Dior seamed stockings in their original box; a purple satin thong glittering with diamanté; a picture of a woman wearing nothing but black silk hold-ups, long black gloves and a Venetian mask – a look which I recreated especially for him.

We'd cook together, maybe visit a museum, walk in the park, talk, play Scrabble, watch TV, have tea and crumpets by the fire and lots and lots of fantastic sex. He even met my younger daughter one Sunday lunchtime when she popped by. It was normal in a crazy kind of way, but I was grounded enough to know that it was what it was and nothing more.

After a while, for no discernible reason, the gaps between our times together began to widen and then things more or less petered out. I accepted this without question or complaint. I loved Ben's company but, when he left, he never took my heart with him. We still speak occasionally and I shall always think of him most fondly. A sexual athlete of impressive proportions, his personal generosity and gentle spirit will always have a treasured place among my souvenirs.

THE GEEZER ERUPTS

Although I was sexually committed and faithful to Ben during our six months together, I was mindful of the fact that it could end at any time. Hedging my bets, I did not cut myself off completely from Keith. I'd told him about Ben – after all, why not? He was in a full-time relationship – why shouldn't I be? I thought it might cool him down but, *au contraire*, it had the opposite effect. Instead of taking a small step back, he took a rather giant leap forward and began to send me some intrusive, slightly voyeuristic emails:

Hi W,
I trust you had a lovely weekend with Ben, not getting out of bed much and all that?!... I actually get a slightly perverted kind of arousal knowing you've been at it with another guy....the fantasy idea of watching you fuck is very sexy and is making me hard as I write my thoughts.

You must tell me what you enjoy with your 'man'. I want to know your preference of men's underwear and pubes: wild, trimmed, porn star stripe or shaven, dress code for a sexy night in or out...this sort of thing. I'm curious and keen to please by way of attention to detail.

To avoid the awful issue occurring, if we get this far...what's your say on protected sex? I absolutely hate condoms, they ruin the heat of the moment, the spontaneity of 'slipping in' for a while and stopping for oral or something else, they feel like you're wearing a wet sock on your cock and they look horrible stuck on the end of an erection... I like seeing my thick, hard cock in motion...not covered in surgical latex. It's a horrible subject to deal with and I'd like your view point.

I've been thinking about you on and off since last time, I play with myself thinking about you every time I need to, which is quite frequently! I imagine you wearing a long, buttoned-up summer dress... heels, sheer tan stockings...purple satin and lace knickers...matching quarter cup bra and suspender belt. You open the door, I step in...we embrace and kiss...I cup your bottom, you squeeze my hardening cock and balls...I unfasten my belt and drop my jeans...you take hold of me as I press against your crotch...gyrating into you.

I unbutton your dress from top to bottom, dropping to my knees as I finish... I push you to the wall, lifting one of your legs over my shoulder... I start eating you through your already moist knickers... You respond in energetic thrusts and bursts of moans and gasps... We can withstand it no longer... I pull your knickers to one side...darting my tongue deep into you to test your wetness... I stand, grabbing your buttocks, you jump up, I plunge deep inside in a single, swift thrust... Your back against the wall, we stand fucking and kissing as the feelings build inside our bodies as we bang, bang, bang with each strong, deep penetrative plunge...

We move to the living-room, I throw you onto your armchair, your legs crooked over the arms... I go down to eat you once more...lapping at your smooth, wet, juicy pussy... You pull at my hair... pulling me up, you grasp at my rock hard cock... you take me into your gasping, hungry mouth... sucking in my whole length pausing only to lick my smooth, circumcised helmet and veined shaft in fits of greed. Your flushed face looks so inviting, I lean and arch my back as my orgasm approaches...you stop suddenly, you stand...pushing me off and into the chair...you straddle me...sinking down onto my cock...you bounce away, your feet on my thighs, your beautiful blonde hair falling over your face...your hands cupping your breasts...your fingers diving beneath the satin and lace to pinch your erect nipples...

You ride me as fast as you can, I pull your bra straps over your shoulders, the cups fall down revealing your pert, naked breasts...bouncing in time with your movements... Your climax nears, you speed, you moan and gasp, you arch your back, your hands fall behind onto my kneecaps, your nails dig in...your mouth open in silent gasps, your eyes fix with mine... I buck, you flinch, I moan, you pull off dropping to your knees, taking my cock into your mouth again... I fuck you, holding your head, pulling your hair, you flick my helmet and bite

beneath the rim as my hot spunk jets over your pretty face...
Perhaps something like this might happen one day.
Notice the lack of 'I paused – you unpacked the condom and rolled it on in a clumsy struggle...' In reality we might have to add this bit!
See you soon.
Love K XX

I must admit I was quite shocked as I read this well-constructed, descriptive and arousing sex scene. It was a shame he wasn't there to act it out with me because although morally I wanted to disapprove, I actually got quite turned on. I would not, however, give him the satisfaction of knowing this as I wished at all times to retain – or at least appear to retain – a façade of ladylike self-control.

I re-read it, dealt as I must with my physical responses, then replied as follows:

You cheeky bastard!!!!
I enjoyed reading this and will reply at length tomorrow when the tiredness wafting over me from my lack of sleep this weekend has abated. Then I can take the time to give you back as good as you gave me...
Just for now, you need to know the following:
1. I do not enjoy rough sex.
2. I like very long, very slow foreplay...
3. You will NOT ever come in, on, or anywhere near my face!
4. The condom question will have to be addressed.
Sleep well if you possibly can after all that typing!
W

The following evening my mood was much more relaxed so I decided to dispense a little sexual largesse his way:

Hi K

Fancy some late night cyber sex? I thought you might...

I've spent a very industrious evening preparing a birthday dinner party for a girlfriend. Sex is not very much on my mind, but I feel I owe you one, although it may not be like for like...

Before I begin, you once mentioned that you have an almost permanent hard-on and that you often pop home 'during the day': is this so your girlfriend can accommodate your needs or is it simply to knock one off? Just curious!

Anyway to answer your questions, here goes:

• I like a well-muscled man with a good, hard body and strong arms, pecs and thighs.

• I like white, grey or black Calvin Klein boxers so I can handle the goods through the soft cotton fabric which I find quite erotic.

• Bushes should be either completely shaved, trimmed very close or 'stripe', definitely not wild, as I hate getting pubes between my teeth necessitating a visit to the dentist for a haircut!

• He doesn't have to have a six-pack, nor a Mr Universe-type oiled physique. This shows too much vanity and attention to himself rather than to me.

• I like to play with a man's silky underarm body hair but I am obsessed with cleanliness and very susceptible to unpleasant smells. A whiff of aromatic after-shave is a turn-on.

• I love nuzzling a young man's neck especially

that part at the nape, which I find very sexy as the skin is smooth and soft.

• I prefer a smooth hair-free butt but I don't mind if it's a little furry.

• Clean well-pedicured feet are essential.

• I like a man with sensitive nipples so I can lick them and sometimes fantasise I'm with another woman.

• I enjoy the power surge I get from giving a great blow job, and believe me, kid, I give a great blow job.

• I also love receiving oral sex. This is an integral part of lovemaking but I rarely give head unless given it first.

• I like doing it on our sides so I can control the movements and ensure my clitoris is involved. My clitoris always needs to be involved!!!!

• I like taking it doggy-style in front of a mirror.

• I like having sex with some clothes or lingerie on. It feels hurried and forbidden like I'm not meant to be doing it – naughtier than being naked. I only go naked when it's very dark or with just a candle flickering!

• I like wearing lace top hold-ups and very high heels with diamanté ankle straps because they make me feel like a whore. I'll dig the heels into his back if he wants me to - or even if he doesn't.

• I don't understand the pleasure women get from anal sex. I've only done it once as a very special favour but there were too many elements which didn't work for me...

• I love having my nipples tongued and sucked but never too hard unless I demand it.

• I quite enjoy 69 but it is often difficult to get the

positioning right. Although I generally prefer taller men, it fits better with a shorter one!

• I rarely let a man come in my mouth - only if I am totally abandoned or feeling very generous.

• I like making love to music, big heartbreak ballads or classical. Mozart's *Requiem* and Ravel's *Bolero* are perfect as they both build up to a soaring crescendo.

• My favourite fantasy is that I am a young nun travelling alone through the night in a storm. I arrive at an inn where there is only one single bed already occupied by a young priest. I plead with the innkeeper and he allows me to enter the room. I remove my wet clothes and slide in beside the novice but the only way to get comfortable is for him to spoon behind me. Inevitably, he becomes aroused. I feel his erection nudging against me and I cannot help but back my buttocks into him. I am very wet and almost imperceptibly, he slips inside me. We try to ignore this at first, until I start undulating slowly back and forth. Our motions synchronise and build until he is slamming into me, biting my neck and clutching my breasts as we revel joyously in the fervour of our first joint orgasm.

Do you know enough about me now? Maybe you know too much...maybe if we get it together it won't be like this at all. Maybe we'll make our own pleasure in our own way.

I'm going to bed now to play with myself. I will lick my middle finger and run it up and down my clit. I will play with my tits and I will come very quickly. Good night!

W xx

Having got myself in a right two-and-eight, I then couldn't wait for his reply which also came quickly:

Wendy... I love what you wrote in reply to mine! In my view we are totally compatible for great erotic, sensual sex as we enjoy the same things... Yesterday I returned home for lunch and pleasured myself...as I'm doing right now... typing with one finger!...imagining you're sucking my nipples as I slowly but deeply penetrate you...but then finishing off doing it doggy...as I love this as much as you!... Can't wait to kiss and undress with you before we shower...I'll have to come over to yours straight from work in my dusty combats...
K xx

In between these emails, Keith called and texted often. He was nothing if not constant and I appreciated this. When Ben went off the radar, as he was wont to do, and I got to feeling frustrated and neglected, Keith was always bubbling away on the back burner. Eventually, weakened by his not so gentle persuasion, I agreed to another date.

He arrived on my doorstep one Wednesday evening straight from work. I'd spent ages getting ready, throwing lingerie and outfits all over the room eventually settling on an ecru lace bra and thong, lace-top stockings and suspenders, a pearl necklace and earrings, and high-heeled cream satin evening shoes. I put a silky, crossover dress on over the top. He texted me that he was running a little late and I poured myself a vodka and tonic. By the time he rang the bell, I was feeling just right, but he was stressed because he hadn't been able to park and his girlfriend had already phoned him twice asking where he was, why he was working late again, and what time he thought he'd be home!

I poured him a glass of wine and winced slightly as he plonked himself down in his work clothes onto my cream silk sofa. He noticed The Look and bounced up again, and I asked him if he'd like to freshen up. He took the hint and went to the bathroom where he spent a good ten minutes splashing about during which time I poured myself another V & T. When he emerged washed, brushed and fully-dressed, I decided to take the initiative and put my arms around him. This felt a little stiff and contrived, but we headed towards each other and into our first kiss. He tongued me deeply which was nice enough, but failed to get me started. He began to stroke up and down my back and I did the same with his, and we graduated to the sofa where we continued kissing and fumbling. Something was not happening, and I pulled away to finish my drink in the hopes that this would crank me up the required seven notches to horny. It didn't.

I took his hand and placed it high on my thigh so that he could feel the suspenders through my skirt. I was sure this would ignite a fire between us. He played awkwardly with my stocking tops for a few moments and then asked if we could 'go inside'. I got up and walked ahead into my bedroom where in three swift moves, he stood naked before me. Young, fit...and totally flaccid.

What, I thought, am I supposed to do with that? I was damned if I was going to perform a song and dance routine to get it to sit up and take notice after he'd been promising me a rampant hard-on for so long. My mere presence should have set him alight but he was clearly very nervous, very guilty, very impotent, or all three. To say I was disappointed was an understatement.

I removed my dress and lay on my bed in the most Sunday Sport pose I could muster. He came towards me and did the decent thing – pulled my panties down and set about satisfying me with his tongue. At least he knew his way around a woman. I probed intermittently between his legs with my toes to see if his ministrations to me had provoked a reaction in him, but sadly, the mouse stayed in the house. I decided to go for it and let myself come. Something to show for my efforts after all!

Once I'd had my orgasm, I completely lost interest. I like to be a generous lover and will usually return an oral compliment, but like an artist, you need something to work with. It wasn't my fault he had the Sword of Damocles hanging over his head instead of between his legs, or maybe he was simply all mouth and no trousers. At this point, certainly – no trousers.

He was obviously very embarrassed and I hugged him to show there were no hard feelings. He explained his guilt vis-à-vis his girlfriend and I gave him a bit of a counselling session. Then he got fidgety as he was running out of time, so he got dressed, said a regretful goodbye and left – an anti-climax if ever there was one. We emailed again a couple of times after that but then it fizzled out – a classic case, yet again, of fantasy being so much better than reality.

Some months later I went to Spain on holiday. Lying round the pool under the sunshade bored with my book and with the female equivalent of a lazy lob, I decided to text him:

...Moist tendrils of hair curl on the back of my neck as a bead of perspiration trickles down between my breasts. I fan my skirt up around my thighs and the air cools me...mmmmm...maybe an ice cube or two...

Immediately I receive back:

Fabulous!! Your simple sentence inspired such delightful thoughts!...and what thoughts!!...thank you, you've just made my cock twinge

Then a second:

I fancy oiling you all over then blindfolding you for a kinky fuck...in every room in the house...

...followed later in the day by an email, which I picked up in the cyber café in town:

Hi W,

I long to be standing with you some hot, sticky summer's evening on a balcony overlooking the sea under the setting sun with a bottle of chilled white wine. You're wearing a delicate sun dress; me: a crisp pressed cotton shirt...we're both clammy and sexually charged...

I stand behind you...running my hands over your bottom, your back...feeling your body beneath the damp cotton... My hands move to your bare shoulders, slipping off the thin straps... I cup your pert breasts, gently kissing and biting your nape...tasting your sweat...my erection pressing into your firm buttocks, resting between your cheeks... Your hands pass round to unbuckle my trousers...you free my thick, hard cock and pull me closer. I slowly unbutton the front of your dress...you feel the breeze over your naked skin...the dress drops to the floor...my hands caress and tease your nipples...sliding down your sweaty torso to your smooth mound and soaking pussy...

My fingers tease you and flit inside... I lift you off your feet as you pull me to enter you from behind... you back onto me as I slide in...just a little...pulling away to make you beg for more...the rhythm slows and speeds as we make love until the sun disappears and the night air chases us inside.

Just an idea...

x

Give this guy an inch and he grew a yard! I daydreamed through this imagery and, in my relaxed holiday state, wandered around town the next day looking for the famous button-through dress he so often talked about. I failed to find one, but so what? We'd played this scene before with no satisfactory conclusion...at least not for him. For my own amusement however, and to while away the hours, I kept up the sex texting (ensuring as always, that, unlike his, my grammar was correct) throughout the holiday:

Me: I wish your head was between my legs

right now. I'm dripping with desire
Him: Just went home for lunch. Felt so
horny, dreamt I was giving you a full body
massage, then you squatted on my face
before modelling the entire contents of
your lingerie drawer!
Me: I'm face down on a lounger offering my
naked back to the Sun God. His rays warm
me as I undo my bikini top and toss it
aside. If you were beneath me now, I would
rub my hot oiled body all over your cool
dry one
Him: you moan as my kisses weave their
magic on your neck and spine. You stand
then pull on my huge erection as you guide
me little by little then grind down slowly
until your soft peach bottom is in my lap
Me: My nipples are erect and I run my
tongue across my lips. Wish it was the
head of your long smooth shaft
Him: you know I'd adore hours of pussy
worship. I now have a raging hard-on. You
insatiable bitch! I'll cup your breasts
and feel my way down to the smoothness
between your parting thighs
Me: You toy with my juices and taste them,
then move behind me and pull me back
against your throbbing...

It was a teenage boy's wet wank, the full fat version of
a Mills & Boon novel...and so on and so forth until it was
time for me to come home.

♀

A few days later, in a different head space altogether, waiting in line to post a parcel surrounded by little old ladies collecting their pensions, my mobile warbled a text alert:

I need you standing in front of me...baby
doll, sheer thong, fluffy heels...one foot
up on the sofa. I kiss, lick and eat you
while I slowly pleasure myself.

Oh get a life! What if one of the little crinklies was peering over my shoulder? She could have had a heart attack!

You're very rude! I replied haughtily. I'm
queuing in the Post Office for God's sake!
Stop this at once! I'm not in the mood!

Which only served to provoke:

Rude is where it's at. Had a fabulous
fantasy in the bath last night: we were
at a party. A pretty, busty young blonde
and her guy started talking to us... you
flirted with them; we drank too much and
you and she started touching. We went
back to their penthouse overlooking the
Thames...shared more champagne, then had
the most liberating fourway sex... I was
fucking you, you were eating her, I was
blowing him, he was kissing your breasts!!

This was received in three separate texts with my mobile going off every few seconds much to the irritation of everyone in the queue.

Have you quite finished?!! I texted back with pursed lips.

Then I thought about it and realised something he'd said had rung my bells. I added:

...although I am rather interested in
seeing u blowing another man...

The queue crept forward inch by elderly inch, and then finally, fifteen minutes later, I heard the four little words I'd been longing to hear:

'Cashier number five, please!'

PLOD

THE MINGING DETECTIVE

My first scream split the still summer night like a siren in a cemetery. The tall trees in the dark park nudged each other and whispered in the wind: watch, watch... A man in the mansion block opposite, dozing, dreaming as the TV droned, rose up sharply from his comfy sofa, stared out the window then dialled 999. The neighbours ran to their balconies, drawn by compulsion to witness the violence unfolding in the street below - live, unedited, action-packed, and more dramatic than anything on the box that night...

I had been to a committee meeting of my singles group at a friend's flat in Hampstead. At 10.30 p.m., with no more to discuss, we gathered up our papers, said our goodbyes and left in our respective cars. I locked my doors as usual, placed the file on the passenger seat and tossed my handbag into the foot well. Driving home, singing along to an old love song on Heart FM, I remembered I needed milk, so I pulled up at the late-night grocer by Maida Vale Station. The bright street and shop lights spread a warm and comforting neighbourhood glow. A couple were kissing on the corner. A woman was property-hunting in the estate agents' window. A dark, bearded man stood smoking by the crossing. The Asian shopkeeper nodded at me as he swabbed the faded lino floor with an old string mop. I bought a pint of milk and a banana for breakfast and returned to my car. This time, I tossed my handbag onto the passenger seat, the plastic carrier on the floor and didn't bother with my seatbelt for the short journey home. Nor did I relock the car doors.

I turned into my road which runs opposite Paddington Recreation Ground, the Rec, as we locals call it. This well-kept park is usually filled with the sounds of leisure and pleasure: strollers chatting, children playing, dogs barking, lovers laughing, runners pounding, tennis balls popping as they pass to and fro across the nets. By day, a green and lively space; by night, a dark, forbidding place. In the fertile months, the trees are at their fullest, obscuring the street lamps as they overhang the road. There is parking along both sides of the street, a boon to us residents – a burden too – for creatures of the night lurk in the undergrowth, concealed by the shadows and the closely-parked cars. Some evenings there are taxis pulling up, people walking their dogs, but that night the street was deserted. Dark and quiet and empty. You could have heard a fox fart.

I pulled into a space on the Rec side of the road, turned my engine off, removed the car key and the front panel of the radio which I hid in its usual place. I leaned over to pick up the committee papers and the carrier bag from the corner shop. I got the keys to my flat ready in my hand and generally faddled around for a bit longer than usual.

Suddenly, with no prior warning, my passenger door was ripped open and a hooded youth in a leather bomber jacket snatched my handbag from the front seat. A voice in my head screamed: 'NO!!!' and without a second thought, I leapt from the car shrieking like a banshee and lunged at him, yelling 'Give that back!' I made a grab for my bag, grappling with one handle while he held on fast to the other. A tug-of-war ensued, during which the bag burst open and some of the contents spilled out into the road. We were pulling and pushing each other as he tried to shake me off but I hung on for grim death. He dragged me backwards across the road and slammed me against a parked car. I lost my grip on the bag but seized the sleeve of his leather jacket, yanking it half off him in my rage and indignation.

And then, in one seamless move, he pulled a gun. He stood before me in classic shooting stance: legs spread, arm outstretched, the weapon clasped, aimed and pointed four inches from my head.

'Let go or I'll use it,' he rasped.

I stared at the gun and three thoughts flashed through my head:

1. That's not real

2. If he shoots me I won't feel anything

3. Oh-my-God-my-children

...and then he hit me.

The first blow to my forehead felled me and I went down heavily onto my left knee, reaching out to break my fall and bending my wrist awkwardly as I crashed to the ground. He stood above me and set about raining blows on the back of my head, pistol-whipping me with the butt of the gun. I could hear a neighbour screaming and sobbing from her balcony: 'Leave her alone...stop it...stop it!' but the sound seemed to come from a long way away. I cowered in the gutter wondering when and how this was all going to end... and then, as swiftly as it had begun, it was over – the whole incident probably lasting no more than forty seconds.

I raised my head and watched him lope off down the street still holding my half-empty handbag. He dragged a bicycle alongside him which he soon mounted and pedalled away. The neighbours who'd rushed out surrounded me but no one went after him. Well, they wouldn't, would they?

Slowly and carefully, they helped me up to standing and I did a mental body check. I wriggled my wrists. Nothing was broken. I looked down. My shoes were missing, my toes grazed and bleeding. One earring and a gold bracelet had gone. I was bleeding from several small wounds, cuts and scratches on both arms and my knee was gashed, a bloodstain spreading like raspberry coulis on my light blue jeans. My head throbbed, I had three broken nails (damn!) but overall, I was OK. I felt strangely elated, victorious, empowered even – not like a victim at all. The neighbours were gathering my belongings from all over the road and bringing them to me like trophies from a battleground: my credit card wallet, my digital diary, my make-up purse, my notepad and pen, and mercifully, both sets of keys.

'You put up a bloody good fight,' said one man, handing me my shoes.

'You OK?' queried another anxiously. 'We've called the police...'

'Did you get a good look at him?' asked the woman from no. 36.

'Do you need an ambulance?' enquired a fourth, touching my arm.

They stood in the roadway all talking at once, everyone giving their account of what they'd seen, their own mugging stories suddenly taking precedence over mine. The couple from the first floor gently led me inside and by the time I reached my flat, the police had arrived. Two uniformed constables and three plain-clothes WPCs stomped into my living-room.

'Anyone fancy a drink?' I asked, retreating into the comfort of hostess mode. 'Tea? Or coffee?'

They shook their heads.

'We don't normally recommend you 'ave a go,' said the main man disapprovingly, 'but it seems you done alright... sure you don't want the 'orspital?'

I declined, but let one of the WPCs bring me a glass of water. For a non-smoker, I sure fancied a cigarette. I made my statement and gave a brief description of my assailant but, annoyingly, not once during the entire fray had I actually looked in his face. I'd looked down the barrel of a gun, oh yes, but not once into the bastard's eyes. Neither had I thought to kick him in the balls or any of that kung-fu stuff you see in the movies. I guess you don't go provoking your mugger once you know he's armed – not unless you're a Charlie's Angel.

A member of the Forensics Team turned up and swabbed my fingernails for DNA. They asked me to let them have my t-shirt which they stored in a plastic bag to test for his fibres. A police photographer arrived and took pictures of all my injuries. I had fourteen separate marks on my body, many more purple, black and blue bruises to appear over the next few days. I gave account of all I could remember, but at 1 a.m., when an officer arrived with a big black photo album, I could say who my attacker wasn't, but I could not, with any certainty, say who he was.

After questioning the neighbours and other witnesses and ensuring that there was nothing more they could do, the police left and I was suddenly alone. I had reached home at 10.40 p.m. and it was now 1.45 a.m. I looked at myself in the hall mirror and asked my reflection:

'What the fuck happened there?' and I waited to break down.

I was desperate to talk to someone but it was late and it didn't seem fair to phone a friend. I ran a bath, dropped in some lavender oil, and slid into the womb-like sensation of the scented water. I washed the dried blood off my wounds, cleaned off my make-up and got into bed. My heart was racing erratically and I had to still it with some deep yoga breathing. Sleep was *hors question*, so I kept the TV on, just for the voices and the company. I dozed on and off, replaying the mugging in my head – fast forwarding, pausing and rewinding it like a video nasty you can't help watching over and over again. I thought about the repercussions and what may have been, and I thanked God for protecting me for my future and my children.

In the morning I awoke completely hyper, on some sort of adrenalin high, emotionally and physically wired. I felt like a beast of the jungle, walking around with my shoulders squared and my fists clenched.

'Come and have a go, you motherfuckers!' I said loudly to no one in particular.

I had expected to faint, cry, throw up or start fitting, but none of these had occurred which was just as well as the day turned into open house at the OK Corral.

As news of the saga spread, people started turning up on my doorstep: my girlfriend Maggi, anxious and tutting with herbal tea and sympathy; the chairman of the residents' association, horrified and commiserative; the porter threatening to 'get the bugger' if he could; a little-known neighbour with a bunch of pink carnations. I really appreciated the attention and was warmed by the genuine care in my hour of need. Just as I managed to ease everyone out the door, C.I.D. at Paddington Green rang up to say a couple of Crime Squad officers were on their way over.

I buzzed them in and they plodded up the stairs. I opened my front door to greet a 6'11" brick shithouse with shoes like coffins followed by a younger, slimmer, shorter man with the cocky air of someone who thinks he's someone. He may have had a point. He looked a bit like Pierce Brosnan. Mmmm, I thought...worth getting mugged for? Although the sleepless night would not have done much for my skin tone, my eyes were bright and shining and I was obviously exuding some kind of animal pheromone.

The two officers sat down on the sofa and accepted coffee. I noticed Little Cop's eyes were everywhere, scanning the room for clues as to my status and demographic. Whether his curiosity was professional or personal was irrelevant. The interest was there. While Big Cop asked the questions, Little Cop's gaze burned into me. I visually included him in all my answers, making eye contact above and beyond the call of duty. He was doing some serious staring and nodding, or maybe he was just being really attentive and sympathetic. Or maybe he had early-onset Parkinson's and a cast in his eye. Or maybe I'd finally lost the plot and thought that every man I came into contact with really, really fancied me.

Once Big Cop had finished taking notes, I asked them a couple of questions about increased crime in the area, how often they patrolled at night, and what the ratio of incident to capture was? We all agreed how, in general, the inner city had become a more dangerous place to live.

'Especially for a woman on her own...' I commented darting a meaningful look at Little Cop.

'Of course you've got some pretty big housing estates nearby. Kilburn, Queen's Park...' Big Cop added as he stood up and gathered his papers together.

'Rough element, I'm afraid...plenty of rich pickings around here and St John's Wood...bit of a happy hunting ground for them...'

They thanked me for the coffee and my time, and Big Cop shook my hand and walked out of the front door onto the common landing. Little Cop lingered a while examining one of my pictures, a print by Pissarro entitled *Place du Théâtre Français, Rain* c.1897. I'd bought it for five quid in a charity shop, varnished it, applied a craquelure finish, had it re-framed and it now looked like an oil painting. He nodded in approval then turned to me and shook hands, holding mine a little longer than was necessary. I wondered what weird and wonderful planetary activity was going on. I was starting to come down from my emotional high, and was feeling a tad wobbly and insecure. It must have shown in my eyes. I needed a hug.

'Be in touch,' he said gently, as if sensing my mood. 'And if you think of anything else – anything at all...give us a call.'

'Thank you, I will,' I nodded and they plodded off back down the stairs. I closed the door behind them and took the coffee cups into the kitchen. A deep sinking feeling of aloneness assailed me and I finally felt the need to cry. I went out onto my balcony for some air and looked down to the street below. They were just leaving the building.

Big Cop got into the driver's seat of the unmarked police car and Little Cop got into the passenger seat. The electric sun roof whirred open and I could see him quite clearly through the opening. As if drawn by my gaze, he looked up and wiggled his fingers in a little wave. I smiled down at him and wiggled mine back.

'Did something just happen there?' Big Cop asked Little Cop as the squad car sped away.

'I'm not sure,' he answered, '...may have done...' and he winked at his colleague in that pig-headed way that men do.

♀

I went wistfully back inside and dialled my best friend, Bernice.

'I don't suppose it's considered appropriate to hit on a member of Her Majesty's Constabulary in the middle of an investigation?' I asked.

'Probably NOT,' Bernice answered firmly. 'And I can only guess why you're asking. Can't you let go for five minutes? You've just sustained a severe beating – you ought to be lying down with a cold compress not chasing uniforms.'

'He's plain clothes actually,' I justified. 'And we definitely had "a moment".'

'Whatever...' Bernice sighed. 'I personally wouldn't touch him with barge pole but if you insist, all I can say is: hang in there, the case will eventually be closed.'

'The sooner the better,' I answered. 'I think I'm in love.'

♀

In the week that followed I had so many messages of solace, sympathy and support from family, friends and neighbours it quite restored my faith in human nature. I was blown away by how kind and thoughtful people could be. I'd reported the story to the local paper, spewing out a garbled account which they printed word for word. A press photographer came round and 'shot' me, posed like an Avenging Supergran next to my car under the headline 'Gunman Mugger Meets his Match'. It made the front page. I developed something of a celebrity status in the neighbourhood. People recognised me when I walked down the street and complete strangers nodded at me in recognition. Some tutted in dismay.

Keen for an excuse to see Plod again, I phoned the police station the following Saturday morning to see if he was on duty. Sure enough he was, so I drove over to Paddington Green with a copy of the newspaper clutched in my hot little hand. I parked my car near Church Street market and walked into the reception of London's hardest cop shop, the one where they take all the terrorists for questioning. I went up to the desk and asked the Duty Sergeant if D.C. Drake was around.

'I was mugged at gunpoint last week,' I explained validating my enquiry, 'and I may have some information for him.'

Winging it as usual, I had no idea what this information might be. I relied on it to come to me before he did, dismissing the fact that I could, of course, have told him over the phone.

The Desk Sergeant made a quick call and before long, Plod burst through the double security doors and crossed the floor towards me. He was shorter than I remembered and looked rather surprised to see me. His hair was tousled like he'd been running his fingers through it (ooh! let me) and he was wearing a pair of jeans, a cream long-sleeved top and suede lace-up boots. He looked cute and dishy.

'Hi!' I began, my voice emerging several octaves higher than I'd intended. 'I was just passing...don't know if you've seen this?'

And I held up the paper for him to look at. The picture showed me standing in the roadway with my hands on my hips and a 'come-and-have-a-go-if-you-think-you're-hard-enough' expression on my face. Plod raised his eyebrows and laughed.

'Blimey!' he said taking the paper from me and scanning the article. 'Good picture...'

'Thanks,' I answered, pleased he thought so. 'I just thought the story might provoke some response...? Or at least help any women out there who read it to be on the lookout when they come home late at night.'

'Yes, any publicity is useful. And someone might recognise the m.o...' he tailed off.

'I was wondering...' I went on racking my brain for an idea which finally came to me. 'I wanted to find out from you if I'm allowed to carry some kind of personal defence...mace or something?'

'Afraid not. It's viewed as an offensive weapon...best thing's a can of hairspray. Keep it in your handbag or your car. And a rape alarm's always useful. You can get them here.'

'Yes...I'll have to get one of those...' I nodded sagely.

People were wandering in and out and a small group of oddballs and vagrants had gathered at the desk. The atmosphere was not exactly conducive to flirting.

'Will you let me know how the investigation is progressing?' I asked grasping for something else to say.

'Of course,' Plod replied. 'But it's not really my case, it's D.C. Dawson's. I just came along for the ride.'

'Oh, OK,' I nodded, disappointment clouding my eyes.

'But I'll get my t-shirt back eventually?' I queried, grasping at...well, t-shirts.

'Sure. But Forensics usually holds on to evidence for a few weeks...'

'That's OK,' I said. 'I doubt if I'll want to wear it again anyway...not exactly my lucky top!'

He smiled.

'Well, thanks for everything,' I said, having nowhere else to go with this conversation. 'Have a good weekend.'

'Stuck here I'm afraid.' Plod replied, and then lowering his voice and leaning towards me, he added: 'Take care.'

We said our goodbyes and I left. Bit of a non-event really, and I drove home feeling deflated and transparent, wondering what on earth had possessed me to pitch up like that. I hoped I hadn't made myself too obvious...

♀

I got all moony for a while every time I heard a police siren in the night, wondering if it was Him on his white steed with the blue flashing light, en route to eradicate evil in the name of the law. I drove past Paddington Green quite often in the course of a normal day, and I knew he was up there somewhere in the ugly concrete tower, bringing a touch of gorgeousness into the lives of the community and his colleagues.

Out of the blue, a few weeks later, I got a call from him. Forensics had finished with my t-shirt and it was available for collection.

'Would you like to pop by and pick it up?' he asked, 'Or I could drop it off to you one evening after work?'

Ooh, tough call.

'Well if it's no trouble...' I answered quickly. 'Could you bring it over?'

'Sure,' he said. 'Probably on Thursday, if I finish on time. Around 7 o'clock?'

'I'll be here,' I replied making a mental note to cancel all social arrangements until further notice.

I hung up the phone unreasonably elated. Delivering back my t-shirt himself? Surely the C.I.D. had better things to do than that? I attached an inordinate amount of importance to his offer and spent the rest of the week hovering somewhere between Clouds Eight and Ten.

On the Thursday I got all dolled up in a casual kind of way, and he arrived on my doorstep just after 7 p.m. My heart was fluttering like a caged canary and he smiled broadly and held out a Tesco bag towards me.

'Come in,' I invited. *Would you like a fuck?*

I actually said 'drink' but I know what I was thinking. He wandered in, relaxed comfortably on my sofa and accepted a Coke. We chatted about this and that, not going anywhere remotely personal now we had the chance. I told him I'd campaigned to Westminster Council for extra lighting in the road and got it organised very quickly. I told him I was ultra-aware when I came home alone at night. I asked him how long he'd been in the force and what was the most exciting thing that had ever happened to him. He told me he'd been stabbed once during an arrest and I made the requisite shocked and sympathetic noises, but overall good manners and decorum prevailed.

'Would you like to take down my particulars?' and 'How big's yer night stick, then?' did not seem appropriate questions at that time. Eventually we ran out of steam and he got up to leave. We shook hands at the door but as he was halfway out, inspiration hit me once again:

'Paul,' I ventured, using his Christian name for the first time, 'I've been really satisfied with the way your department's handled the case' (*I suppose a shag's out of the question?*) 'and I wondered if there was any way I could thank the police' (*and you in particular*) 'for the way you've looked after me during all this?'

'It's our job,' he answered, 'but if you want, you could make a donation to the Widows and Orphans' Fund. There's a collection box at the front desk.'

'OK,' I said, delighted to have another go at stalking him. 'I'll sort something out. Thanks again for popping round.'

And he left.

Being nothing less than tenacious, I immediately wrote out a cheque for £25.00 and attached it to a thank-you note personally addressed to him. Unfettered by the burden of eye contact, I ended the note: '...and if you ever fancy getting together again once the case is closed, I'd be happy to buy you an off-duty drink.'

My personal note cards are 250 gsm thick. The excuse was tissue thin, but blinded by infatuation I went back to the cop shop the following Saturday afternoon in the vague hope of running into him again. Unfortunately for me, a gaggle of immigrants, asylum seekers and people who'd had their pockets picked at the local market were all queuing up at the front desk ahead of me. Didn't these people realise that my case was every bit as important as theirs? I had a member of the Met to seduce, and if we didn't get it together soon, thus improving his private life beyond all measure, he may not be able to conduct himself in a brave and fearless fashion when out in the field in the line of duty!

Eventually, I got fed up waiting, dropped the envelope in the Collection Box and skulked off home as dry as a nun's crotch and twice as disappointed.

I thought about Plod quite a lot in the few weeks that followed, but life took its usual twists and turns and I soon forgot all about him.

Almost one year to the day later, I found myself staying overnight on business at the Thistle Hotel, Middlesbrough (don't ask...). It was evening and I'd eaten a tasty, though solitary, Thai meal in the hotel restaurant. Not wishing to sit alone in the lounge to be eyed up by a greyness of travelling salesmen, I wandered into the hotel's business centre to check my emails. And whaddya know? Amongst the spam, jokes, friendlies and business stuff, there was one from a name I didn't recognise. I almost deleted it, but as I began to read, my jaw dropped onto my chest and I sat there staring at the screen thanking the Guardian Angel of Sex-Crazed Mug-ees for showing me the favour of her grace and mercy.

It was from Plod, apologising profusely for the delay in expressing his appreciation for the donation, explaining that he'd been away on secondment in the Gulf, and wondering whether, twelve months on, the offer of a drink was still available. I could not have remembered his name if I'd been tortured by the Taleban, but I did remember how he'd made me feel, and that memory oozed down my spine like a ladleful of warm treacle. I returned his email immediately, short and to the point:

Hi Paul,
I was very surprised to hear from you after so long, but it would be great to get together when time and geography allow.
Stick that in yer helmet, pig boy.

He replied the next day. Chatty emails passed back and forth between us during the ensuing week and we eventually arranged to meet at the Metropolitan pub in

Notting Hill for the first England game of Euro 2004. I like nothing more than a first date, but this was nothing like the sort of first date I was used to.

I am, and always have been, a football whore. I'll support the team of whichever bloke I'm with or occasionally the opposing team in order to create conflict if I think it's needed. My father and sister were Spurs, I was Arsenal. They were Oxford, I was Cambridge. When I lived with a Chelsea supporter, it was Up The Blues, and when I dated a Liverpool fan, I made sure he'd Never Walk Alone. (I wanted to make sure he'd Never Walk Again, but that's another story.)

On the afternoon of our date at the pub, I texted Paul:
Could you please meet me outside? I don't fancy walking into testosterone city on my tod.
The fact was I could barely remember what he looked like and I didn't fancy fighting my way through the heaving throng and throw my arms round the wrong bloke. As I parked my car I was excited that my plan had come full circle. How many women get mugged and end up dating the investigating detective? (Quite a few apparently, I learned later. Coppers are notorious womanisers and will screw anything on offer because they can. Uniform=sex appeal=power.)

Paul was waiting outside, dressed in jeans and a white linen shirt. He looked good enough to eat. It was a fine afternoon and we went into the beer garden for a drink before the match. He was a very different man to the one on duty, and wasted no time steaming in. He declared his feelings for me at once, saying he'd fancied me all along, but couldn't have done anything about it while the case was under investigation. I was delighted that my instinct had proved right. Plus I'd made it pretty clear how I felt. He'd only had to take the bait.

Once the match kicked off, we squeezed back inside the pub and found somewhere to stand where we could see the big screen. I was drinking vodka and tonic, he was into his lager – but even more significantly, he was well into me. As it was so crowded, we had to stand really close together and soon found ourselves whispering intimately into each other's ears in that sexually-charged way that only takes place at the very beginning of a new relationship. Or in my case, after two vodka tonics. He was extremely talkative and tactile, and at one point he lifted up my hair and began stroking the back of my neck.

'That's what I wanted to do first time I saw you,' he confessed.

And then he told me about his colleague asking: 'Did something just happen there?'

Every woman wants to talk endlessly about 'how did you feel the first time we met' and here he was offering me all the answers on a plate. He interspersed his conversation with loving smiles and lots of stroking. As the game heated up and the pub filled up, we became squashed together and he positioned himself protectively behind me with his arms around my waist. I leaned back against him enjoying every minute. We became very close very fast, but, in fairness, I told myself, I had known him for a year. By the time the match was over, there seemed little doubt where the evening was headed.

We left the pub after a hideous defeat: England had stayed on top for ninety minutes and then came second, rather like the perfect lover. We walked arm in arm to my car and got in.

'Should I be driving?' I asked, putting the key in the ignition and trying to sound like a sober and responsible citizen. 'With you in your current job 'n all?'

'It's not me who's driving,' he laughed running his hand up and down my leg. 'You'll be the one to get done.' Sooner the better, I thought.

'I am definitely over the limit,' I confessed.

'So drive carefully,' he advised and leaned over to smooch my neck. I started the car and crawled carefully home.

We made our way quickly up the stairs and as soon as we were in the door, we fell upon each other. Our first kiss was ravenous and I could hardly believe that what I'd hoped for was finally happening. We were hungry in more ways than one but now I had him in my clutches, I wanted to savour him. I dragged him into the kitchen where I prepared some scrambled eggs and smoked salmon. He distracted my labours continuously with a lot of groping and neck nuzzling. We ate hurriedly then went back to the living-room, onto the sofa and finally into each other's arms. It was all very steamy but I somehow managed to remain partly-clothed and not to give myself up completely. He seemed rather surprised at this, but respected my wishes, mindful perhaps of his position and the way we'd met, and also the unlikely possibility of me crying rape. I was gagging for him but also wanted to extend the seduction and not appear too easy.

More importantly, I'm addicted to firsts and once they become seconds, they lose something of their early edge.

At around midnight, obeying some hastily-written new set of rules, I reluctantly sent him home. He'd be back, I reasoned, and the looking forward would make it all the better. I went to bed churning and yearning wondering what the next day would bring. I was not disappointed. I received an early Good morning x text which pasted a smile all over my face, and he continued texting and phoning me throughout the week. I switched my radio on to Heart FM and sang along to all the love songs like the happiest woman in the world.

We arranged our next date for the following Friday evening. With dogged self-belief and unwavering tenacity, I repeated my mantra: *I'm not going to sleep with him...I'm not going to sleep with him...* From experience, I knew that whatever developed, this was the best time in any relationship and I was determined to make it last as long as possible. Once he'd got what he wanted, he'd be bound to move on. And why rush through the delicious thrill of anticipation, the promise of possibility, the tantalising torment of shall I-shan't I? We all know the minute you've climbed the mountain and admired the view the only way is down. That heady expectation is gone forever and can never be repeated – at least not until you break up and make up, and that only lasts five minutes before it all goes wrong again.

For some self-delusional reason, I had high hopes for Paul and me over and above a one-night stand. Since he was borderline suitable – aged forty with a proper job – I wanted to see if I was capable of nabbing myself an actual boyfriend. So far, he'd behaved impeccably and in my optimistic ignorance I thought there may be an outside chance of this turning into something more than a quick shag. That Friday, he was taking me out for dinner and when he called me that afternoon to say he'd been very busy and hadn't had time to book anything yet, I was understanding and unconcerned. 'I'll sort something out, don't worry,' I offered. We could have eaten at a workman's caff on the Isle of Dogs for all I cared, the man could do no wrong. And at least he'd *intended* to make a booking. That was the main thing.

You can always tell by the contents of my fridge whether or not I've got a man in my life. I buy lager and, on this occasion, there was six-pack of Carling cooling on the top shelf. It made me feel all warm and fluffy when I saw it there and every time I opened the fridge, the lager winked at me and blew me a kiss. At 7.45 p.m., ready and waiting, I did some yoga and sat on the floor in lotus position repeating my affirmations: *I'm not going to sleep with him...I'm not going to sleep with him...I'm not going to sleep with him...*

He arrived with a cheeky smile on his face and a bottle in his hand wrapped in emerald-green tissue paper. He looked very spruce and smelt gorgeous. He reached for me possessively as he walked in the door and gave me a big hug and kiss.

'It's great to see you again,' he said, handing me the bottle.

When I unwrapped it, I saw it was Laurent-Perrier champagne. Blimey! How incredibly stylish! I reached for two crystal flutes and my bottle of cassis, and we toasted each other with promise in our eyes. As we sat chatting, every now and then he'd lean over and kiss me, or stroke my cheek. We were holding hands the entire time.

When I am without someone for a while, I just get on with it, growing a little harder and tougher by the day. I was anxious not to get hurt again, thinking I had surrounded myself with a fortress with walls thick and strong. It didn't take much for the castle to collapse, however, and the 'drawbridge' to fall open. Each look, every touch made me feel treasured and wanted. Yet I had to try to remain in control. There was a moment on the sofa when Paul took the glass from my hand and put it down, then held me very tightly against him, stroking my hair. I could feel his heartbeat next to mine and our passion rose like champagne bubbles to the surface. I wanted him so much I could hardly breathe. I made myself pull away and stared into his soft, brown eyes:

'Paul?' I said, the seriousness clear in my voice. 'I want to ask you a question. Can you describe to me exactly how you feel right now?'

He rose to this verbal challenge with an articulacy and aplomb that quite surprised me.

'Exhilarated, excited, elated, desirous, all my senses are heightened...'

Wow! I couldn't have done better myself.

'Paul,' I repeated – lovingly saying his name again, 'you know right now is the best time? We will never feel this way again...it's very fleeting. I've been thinking about you and looking forward to seeing you, but I'd like to get to know you a little better before we go any further.'

No wonder men never understand women. My virtual legs had been wide open since the moment we'd met and now it was crunch time, I'd slammed them shut.

'We both know the ultimate destination,' I continued, warming to my lecture, 'but once we get there, everything changes. Can't we just relish the foreplay a little longer... I mean, why take the fast train when we can enjoy the scenic route?'

He looked slightly bemused, as well he might. He smiled and kissed me again, weakening the dubious determination of my previous words. He tipped the last of the champagne into our glasses, and we toasted again. He was silent, pensive, probably wondering when exactly he was going to get his shag. At 9.15 p.m., with a 9.30 p.m. table reservation, I said:

'Shall we cancel the table?' completely going back on my

earlier resolve.

'No,' he answered, 'let's go and eat.'

He was now playing me at my own game. We walked hand-in-hand down to the Warrington and had a meal upstairs at Ben's Thai. He talked about his early life, and I found him a sensitive man who didn't mind expressing his emotions. Twice divorced like me with a couple of kids, he admitted his career was not conducive to maintaining relationships. Mmmm...I thought...thanks for the warning. He also repeated that when he'd left my flat after that first interview, he'd wanted to kiss me goodbye, and we laughed about that and the wave we'd shared when he drove off.

After dinner, we came back home and continued our soft seduction of each other. We kissed and cuddled and stroked and teased and danced and drank and gave each other long, lingering looks. He lay on top of me fully-clothed and I held him as close as I could without flesh touching flesh. There was a powerful emotion between us – lust I suppose – but I felt I could easily fall in love. I wondered, if I'd asked him, if he could too... Kenny Rogers sang *Lady* and I tried to be, but the woman in me wanted him and wanted him now. At 2 a.m., my body yearning but my resolve intact, there was only one place for him to go: home. For that night, enough was enough.

I cleared up and went to bed happy, but I couldn't sleep. At 3.30 a.m., I drifted off with a smile on my face and woke again at 6.30 a.m. with the same expression.

I didn't hear from him on the Saturday but I knew he was out of London and luckily I was busy too. I typed out a text saying: Thank you for a magical evening.

The best is yet to come... but I didn't send it. I would have liked to have received that from him and just after midnight, as I was dropping off to sleep, my message beep went off.

Am in a nightclub in Cambridge. Hope you've had a good day. X

I replied magnanimously Have fun. Hope the girls aren't too pretty and I went to sleep. His reply at 1.22 a.m. woke me, but I had left my phone on just in case.

None as pretty as you xxx he said.

Bless, I thought, and I snuggled back down as peaceful as a baby.

On the Monday he invited me to join him and his workmates to watch the next England game which was on that night. I *was* going to my yoga class but, obviously, this invitation took precedence. When I got to the Chapel pub off Edgware Road, it was obvious he'd told them all about me. They were a friendly, gregarious bunch and I felt at home immediately. Paul was very touchy-feely in front of them all and that made me feel fantastic. I couldn't remember the last time I'd been in mixed company with a man who was so obviously keen on me and not afraid to show it. When I got back from the loo at half-time, I felt they'd been talking about me as it all went quiet, and he told me later they thought I was 'gorgeous'. To cap it all England won 4-2!

After the game, we left the pub and he asked if I wanted to go somewhere to eat. I thought about this for a moment but then I offered to cook for him at home which he accepted. We ate some pasta then I shooed him out the kitchen so I could clear up. When I joined him in the living-room later, he was fast asleep on the couch. I guess a few lagers after a hard day's work would do that to a man. I sat down and stroked his hair and he half woke up and looked at his watch. It was 11.15 p.m.

'I have to go,' he yawned. 'I'm knackered...'

I sighed deeply and thought about it. I couldn't bear for him to leave.

'If you promise to be good,' I said slowly, 'would you like to sleep in *my* bed?'

The daftness of some of my questions never ceases to amaze me.

Paul went into the shower and I got undressed and put on a nightie and a pair of clean pants. Saga Home Insurance – very safe, very competitive. He emerged from the bathroom still wet and tousled, my fluffy, burgundy bath sheet wrapped round his waist, his torso glistening as the droplets dried. His body was smooth, hairless and begging to be adored. My knickers were already starting to feel *de trop*. He dropped the towel at the side of the bed and I averted my gaze. We lay down beside each other and began to hug and kiss, his hands stroking my back, lifting my hair as he suckled my neck. I loved the feel of this man alongside me, knowing he was urgent for me, but still, I really wanted to wait. As his ardour rose and along with it my blood pressure, I began to feel guilty and questioned my own motives which were clearly all about control. It's the last bastion a woman has over a man.

Paul began to descend the length of my body, his tongue lapping at my flesh, and I didn't know how I could reasonably stop him. And it seemed juvenile now anyway, the end result was going to be the same, sooner or later. His head was now between my legs, his hands cupping my buttocks as he teased me through my panties.

I suddenly tensed and sat up, pushing him away from

me, thinking: No! I do *not* want to do this yet! I turned to him and took his hand.

'Next time,' I whispered. 'I promise you...next time...'

'You can't say that,' he answered tetchily. 'It puts too much pressure on...' and I realised the battle was all but lost.

I leaned forward in the bed hugging my knees and dropped my head down between them. He fell back against the pillow and let out a frustrated sigh. He was now wide awake and clearly angry. Oh for God's sake, I told myself, what's the difference? This time, next time, sometime, never...you could get hit by a bus tomorrow. He could get shot!

In one move, I pulled my nightie off over my head, dragged my knickers down and threw them across the room. Then I turned to him. I gazed lovingly at his naked body – this delicious, fervent, eager, erect man lying next to me.

I put one hand firmly on his chest to keep him in place and I straddled him, placing my lips against his mouth. I kissed him deeply and juicily then dipped my head and slithered down the length of him flicking my tongue across his nipples, his torso, his taught hard belly. He drew his breath in sharply and let it out again in a hard sigh, this time it was with relief and anticipation.

He left me at 7 a.m. He'd showered quickly and sat on the edge of the bed as he tied his boot laces. He kissed me tenderly and whispered 'Speak to you later' and I listened to the front door slam. I reached over to the empty space where he had lain, and wriggled across the bed to take his place. I repressed the hormonal moment of sadness and went back to sleep.

Later that day, he texted me:

What a wonderful night! Thank you. I feel
very lucky xx

...and, again, all was well in my world.

I didn't hear from him again that day or most of the next.
I was deeply obsessing by this time, banging on to anyone
who'd listen about our night together and how I wished I
hadn't let him have his way so soon. Late on the second
day, I got: We'll be at The Chapel for a 7.30
kick off. Wanna come?

So now I was one of the boys, but phew! What a relief!
Never had an invitation to watch football in a pub thrilled
me so much. It would have been quite clever of me to have
answered: Sorry. I'm busy but did I? Well, would
you?

It was the same scenario with the work mates, the
drinking and the touchy feeling...but something was
different. I knew it would be. The anticipation had
gone and he waited until the end of the evening to tell
me that his friend, Ryan, was staying the night at his. It was
the anniversary of my mugging and it would have been a
sweet irony to have spent it with him...When I mentioned
this, he just said: 'Yea, but you're over that now, aren't
you?'

I drove home in a deep trough convinced that I'd blown
it. He probably thought I was just like all the rest, an
old slapper who pretends to be coy and virginal but is
patently not. No amount of playing hard-to-get makes
a good goddamn once they've had you. I was very pissed
off. He'd picked me up, whirled me around, got my
organs in a tizz then dropped me in a heap to rebuild

myself. *Comme tous les autres*. Maybe if he'd told me at the outset that he would only be mine until the dawn I could have prepared myself. Men should be more honest. They should say: 'Look, I really fancy you and I want to shag you once, but when I'm done you won't see me again.' Then we could make a controlled decision to either say 'Fuck off!' or 'OK. Fine'. We could handle ourselves like they do without any emotional investment. That way we wouldn't be fucked up for the next six months wondering why on earth they haven't phoned.

I heard nothing from him the next day, and although I may have been wrong to write him off so quickly, that powerful old sixth sense told me something was amiss. I was tempted to send a text saying: I had you down as a real charmer but you are, of course, just another bastard but it seemed a bit snipey. And premature.

On the Saturday, I spent the morning preparing a picnic for ten friends, as we were all off to an open air concert at Leeds Castle. It was mid-June, Wimbledon was on and it was, of course, pissing with rain. In between making sandwiches and slicing vegetables for the crudités, I got a nothing text from him which said: Working today. Shame about the weather.

I was tempted to reply: Fuck the weather. Shame about our relationship. Short eh? Just like your dick — but I refrained.

Three days passed and my mood rotted and developed gangrene. One minute he was all sexy texts like: Id really like to corrupt you xxx and the next I'm deafened by the silence. What the hell was he doing every night? His ironing?

♀

There were days when I convinced myself it was over and I didn't really care, and other days, fuelled by alcohol and misery, when I was absolutely desperate to hear from him again. And then suddenly, with no discernable timetable or agenda, he'd send me a chatty text and my world would spin on its axis, do a triple salto and land beautifully with one leg extended elegantly behind it. But no suggestion of a date. Just told me what he was up to and nothing else. I replied in kind and eventually managed to sprat an arrangement out of him by telling him that my aunt had died (true) and I was very upset (she was 94...). He sent me a lovely, caring cyber hug followed by the long-awaited words: Tomorrow night? and I was flying again.

The next afternoon he cancelled: ...there are new prisoners in and its all gone manic.

Yeah, well, whatever...thanks for fucking me *and* my brain. I texted him back way too sycophantic:

Don't worry, honey, I respect what you do, hope to c u soon

...when what I should have put was:

U diss me one more time, you short-arsed cunt, and I'll personally come round and rip your bollocks out through your throat.

Three days later I got another one from him saying: Sorry. Life is hectic. I'll keep in touch.

This seemed promising when I received it, but once I'd re-read fifteen times, it actually sounded like a polite kiss off.

Six days went by with nothing from him at all. Denial gave way to fury, then hurt, guilt, blame, recrimination, jealousy, hope, despair, depression and a deep, visceral sadness. The ten stages of bereavement. Misery and desolation spread through my veins, seeping into every crevice of my being and filling each empty space with a disillusioned longing. I tried to pull myself together and kept as busy as possible, but the pain was present *all the time*. I was obsessing as only a woman can.

I interpreted his silence in all the usual ways: busy at work, gone to see his daughter for the weekend, on night duty, been shot through the head in an ambush. You name it, I excused him for it. But deep down I knew I was fucked. The bastard had got his leg over and that was all he'd wanted. I managed to spend one entire evening with a girlfriend without mentioning him once which was progress, but it didn't mean I wasn't thinking about him.

And then at 11.45 p.m. one night, after a whole week of inner dementia, I received this little nugget:

Sorry haven't been in touch. Been thinking about you though, would love to do what I've been thinking! hope you're well x

Well? Was I well? Well I was now. But also, mixed in with the feelings of euphoria, elation, forgiveness and relief, I felt abused. Cheeky fucker! I was flattered he still wanted me (why did I devalue myself so much?) but deconstructed, the message was no more than a drunken request for sex. And worse still, it could have been directed at anyone! I had no intention of replying until I had thought long and hard about this. I spent most of the night composing different varieties of answer and by morning had come up with what I considered the perfect reply:

A midnight text requesting sex? I'm not
impressed with your communication skills.
Do you honestly think you can dip in and
out of me like a packet of crisps? Go
straight to jail. An officer you may be...
a gentleman you're not!

I saved it but decided not to send it. Not yet. Let him
stew in his own juice.

I spent the next day shopping, cooking and preparing for a
dinner party and I didn't think of Plod all day. Well I did, of
course, as many times as there are seconds in a minute, but
not in an obsessively bad way. Just pondering really: what
was he playing at? What was I playing at? Who does he
think he is? Who did I think I was? You may as well have
asked the moon why it was blue. The dinner party went
well and just before the guests left, I cornered my friend
Karina in the kitchen and ran the text past her. Send it!
she bellowed into my face. Send it now! So I did. I then
re-read it forty times and interpreted it differently each
time.

In the cold light of the next day, I regretted it and spent the
day composing backtracks like:

Message received and misunderstood? or
Maybe I shouldn't have had that 4th vodka or
Was I perhaps a little too harsh?

By the evening, with no response from him, I was again
convinced I'd totally blown it. I was sitting out on my
balcony next evening thinking of sending him a casual
Fancy a drink? when I suddenly got a message from
him. My heart leapt when I saw his name in my inbox and

I read the three little words I'd been longing to hear...

No, dear reader, not I Love You but Fancy a shag?

On the one occasion I really should have given this some thought, my idle thumb inadvertently zapped into action. Without hesitation, or even a vague attempt at being cool and elusive, I immediately replied Yes, totally undermining my cleverly-worded reprimand of the night before. I assumed he would come right over, so I engaged 'manic mode' on my maintenance gearbox and showered, shaved, moisturised and changed in readiness for his imminent arrival. One hour later, not only was he *not* on my doorstep with a dozen red roses, he hadn't even replied to my eager beaver text.

Just to show you quite how stupid a woman in lust can be, I waited. Not exactly patiently, it has to be said...but I waited. And while I waited I drank, I smoked, I paced, I changed clothes and lingerie twice and eventually at about 10.20 p.m. he texted me: Not looking good. May be too late.

Well Fuck You up the Arse with a Giant Cactus, you Shithead Pig Bastard!

Instead of just not replying thereby causing him confusion and maybe gaining a brownie point or two, I sent him the most doormat message ever composed by a woman of cultural standing:
Don't worry. Just get here when you can. If I'm asleep climb in beside me and wake me up. I can't be more accommodating than that.

He didn't even have the grace to reply. At around midnight, having craned my neck so far out the window I now resembled an African tribeswoman, I went to bed.

With all my clothes and my make-up on.

At 00.45 a.m., glory be to God, my doorbell rang. I got up and buzzed him in. He slouched in through the door tired and hungry. I made him a mushroom omelette and some tea and toast and while he was eating, I ran him a nice, hot bubble bath, lit some incense, put on some classical music and led him gently by the hand into my bathroom. We undressed and climbed in together. I massaged his aching feet, his shoulders and his back. I washed his hair then I got out of the bath and left him to relax, sink and soak in the scented suds.

It was a hot July night. I went out onto the little balcony off my bedroom wrapped in my towel, and I stood looking up at the silent moon. It looked down at me reproachfully but I shrugged in my defence. Give me a break, man. I'm only a woman. And it doesn't take much to make me happy. A little crumb of affection...an hour of someone's time...

Memory is indeed selective and I didn't want to spoil the evening by dwelling on what he'd put me through. Or what I'd put myself through. He was here, and this was now, and we had what was left of the night before us.

I heard him emerge from the bathroom but I stayed where I was. He stepped out onto the balcony and pulled my towel away, dropping it with his onto the bedroom floor. He stood behind me and wrapped his arms around my naked body, caressing my breasts and breathing in my hair. I cared not a jot for the neighbours as we stood together bathed in moonlight, the trees rustling in the communal gardens between the mansion blocks. I leaned my head back against his shoulder and sighed deeply at the feel of him and I was Princess Stardust in the Magic Kingdom with her Long Lost Prince.

He led me back inside to my bed and made love to me

with such exquisite tenderness my heart all but broke. When dawn crept all too soon into our private world, the magic melted as I knew it must. He got up early and showered, and came back into the bedroom wearing The Robe.

Embroider your name on the sleeve with the others, I reflected silently, and that gave me a certain satisfaction.

I got up, made myself decent and set about cooking him a full English breakfast. Some of my school reports used to say: must try harder. This one should have said: trying way too hard. He ate gustily then went off to get dressed while I cleared up. We hadn't talked much. There wasn't much to say. In my heart, he was already gone. He came to say goodbye as I stood at the sink, and I turned to face him. I pulled off the Marigolds and looked right at him. He'd seen that look before, that fear of abandonment, that moment of parting, my vulnerability as raw as an open wound. This time it must have scared him, the unspoken question: when will I see you again?

'Thanks,' he murmured as he kissed me on the cheek.

'Bye,' he mumbled as he walked down the stairs.

And I knew as sure as eggs is eggs that I would never see him again...

♀

A year later, on 7/7, the day of the London bombings, the Edgware Road station bomb went off just yards from his office. I texted him: Hope you're OK. Sorry for you and all your colleagues and he replied straight back: Thanks. Not the best of days.

I was over him by then. He'd got what he'd wanted and, up to a point, so had I. Not for long enough...but hey...it would have ended sooner or later.

I like having a C.I.D. officer's private number stored in my mobile. You know what they say about coppers...you can never find one when you want one.

EYE-CANDY ANDY

WHAT YOU CAN GET ON THE INTERNET

'My God! You're gorgeous!' What an amazingly flattering greeting from a man eighteen years my junior! This is how it came about.

Uncharacteristically, I was spending a Saturday night home alone – something I like to refer to as a Me date. I've only just learned how to do this. There's something inside me left over from my teens that says if you're not in Leicester Square on a Saturday night, you don't really exist. (This of course is rubbish. Leicester Square is now a motley *mélange* of tourists and empty burger cartons) So given that the media now tells us that staying in is the new going out and Thursday is the new Tuesday, Saturday nights in have become quite the thing.

So there I was, somewhere between *The X Factor* and *Millionaire*, leafing back and forth through my diary, when I noted that all my Benjamins appeared to have gone AWOL.

In a lull between programmes, I suddenly remembered a website I needed to check out: www.handbag.com, on which I presumed you could buy (cue Lady Bracknell) 'A hend behg?' I was looking for a designer bargain so I logged on and instantly found myself inextricably linked to www.datingdirect.com.

Now I've spent the last two decades trawling life's highways and byways and I've travelled some none too scenic routes in my eternal quest for lurve, but strangely enough, I'd never tried internet dating. Whooaahh! No wonder it's so popular! Before I knew it, I was scrolling through pages and pages of 'kind, generous, animal-loving, solvent, tactile NS men with a GSOH all desperate for a LTR or more'. The single saddos of Olde London Towne were alive and well and living in Leyton, sat at home at their computers, furiously tapping away in a futile attempt to get laid before it got too late. And I understand this now, it's an ACD: addictive, compulsive and disorderly, borne out of the foolish belief that the love of one's life must be out there somewhere with a litre of bourbon in one hand and a Walther PPK in the other, and if you don't find him by the next mouse click, he's going to swig the entire bottle then blow his brains out.

So for the purposes of, ahem, 'social research' I found myself posting up my most alluring photo with the following profile:

> I am a vibrant, vivacious, worldly, erudite, philosophical, feisty, fabulous woman so why am I doing this? I logged on to handbag.com to buy a handbag and found myself linked to this site. I

know, I thought – I'll buy a boyfriend...someone to walk in the park with, someone to dance in the dark with...a confident, self-sufficient, single sweetheart who knows how to live well. Nerds, nutters and Norman-no-friends need not apply. I like younger men who like older women but don't try to mess with my head. I am humorous, glamorous, and give great company but you have to know which buttons to press. Tough call? Maybe...but it'll sort out the men from the boys...

Before you could say 'Didn't you used to be Jack Robinson?' I had received a clutch of replies: a ragbag of cheaters and chancers all fancying an uncommitted dalliance with an attractive, older woman. Some admitted to 'late fifties but young at heart' but in fairness, I too had lied about my age...well, I was hardly going to tell the truth, was I?

I mucked about for a minute or two (forty-seven actually) and just as I was about to log off convinced that this particular Highway to Heaven was not the route for me, there appeared on my screen a 41-year-old hazel-eyed, fair-haired intellectual with his own home, car, hair and teeth and several emails later, I was in a relationship. Like I said before: Whooaahh!

He began:

So you're a national authority on older women/ younger men. How about that. Fascinating stuff... How did you, er, get into that field? You look too young yourself, for a start. (And I am obviously too old!) And in relation to what you were saying about the mind being the most erogenous zone, I might have thought you'd go for the more mature guy? Anyway, I am fascinated and would love to hear more.

To which I replied:

An older man with a younger woman is obviously the norm, but there is a clear social shift going on. And if a relationship works, it works – irrespective of the ages of the participants. Although it doesn't tend to last, there are some successes and think of the fun you'll have along the way. With so much divorce amongst 'same age' couples, one has to look for alternatives. Most men like older women anyway as there is this 'teacher/pupil' dynamic going on.

And he said:

You are rampantly sexy in a sophisticated and thoroughly ladylike kind of way. Also beautiful, intelligent, have boundaries and we're actually communicating. Not bad! Hey, it's all fantasy at this point anyway...but I am finding it fun. And I haven't used you or let you down because I am feeling horny and want to manipulate you into bed. Fantastic.

On a scale of Juan to Den, this worked for me. Andrew, for such was his name, was 6'2", an articulate, funny, well-bred, educated, single, unencumbered man with a seductive dark side. (Despite years of being brain fucked, I still like a man with a seductive dark side!) E-chatting to him was like drinking Heineken: he was reaching the parts other men had long since failed to reach.

Through the days that followed, a powerful mental connection was established, fuelled by a diet of emails and phone calls of the two-hour bedtime variety, in that twilight netherworld when you lower your defences and reveal much more than you know you should. One night, I nearly lost him. I was feeling a bit down and my tough bitch–diva image fell away to reveal a vulnerable, needy woman cowering beneath. This must have freaked him out as he stated quite categorically that if I was looking for long-term commitment, he was not The One. This, of course, egged me on... *I'm gonna make you love me – yes I will, yes I will...*

Another night we got inordinately close to having phone sex (I know he was) and the inevitable rendez-vous was merely a toss away. Our minds had met – how soon our bodies? From experience, however, I was deeply apprehensive about this. Although we had fashioned the perfect fantasy and I actually felt I had a 'boyfriend', I also knew that stepping outside the box into the real world would certainly change things, and not necessarily for the better. The ethereal auto-eroticism was fulfilling most of my needs. Andrew told me he thought about me constantly, loved the sound of my voice, was stimulated by our lengthy dialogues and as an artist wanted to paint me. What the hell else did I need? No one was invading my space, giving me grief, or leaving wet towels all over the bathroom floor, and so we continued to discuss maybe meeting or maybe never meeting.

Him: Perhaps we should keep it like this as you say! You bring out the best in me!

Me: Men usually bring out the best in me too... rapidly followed by the worst...!

In that multi-tasking way that women have, I was able to focus on him, the object of my affections, 24/7. I could have done this whilst mounting a hostile takeover, moving house, dealing with elderly relatives, awkward children, two flat tyres and a lost credit card, and still found time for tea. I also found myself creating fanciful little scenarios in my head which had no way of standing up in real life. As Stendhal said:

> Love has very little to do with the beloved person and everything to do with the lover's imagination. Nothing is so seductive as our own thoughts; the passion that sweeps us off our feet is our own.

Eventually, after about four weeks of this la-la nonsense, it suddenly stopped working for me. This 'relationship', like all my past 'relationships', now had to be rushed through and out the other side. And so I pushed for a meeting which was finally arranged for the following Saturday evening at his home, at which time he would, as promised, sketch or paint me.

The anticipation of this first (and possibly last) date gave me the opportunity to clamber onto an even higher cloud in the Cuckoo Land I now inhabited. I imposed upon myself a week-long regime of self-denial and physical abuse. Semi-starvation to get my stomach flat consisted of a fruit and veg only detox diet which left me raving and craving (chocolate, of course, what else?). To look fit and fabulous: full body exfoliation, deep-tissue massage, hours of diligent fake tanning during which I had to walk around naked like I'd lost my horse and both water melons, a sphincter-clenching Hollywood waxing, manicure, pedicure, highlights, pelvic floor lifts, push-ups, stretches, *kvetches*, underarm shaving, nipple and eyebrow plucking, morning and night-time applications of a new gel called Face Lift (at £33? I don't think so...). And what had he done in the run-up to our meeting? Scratched his balls and bought some condoms probably – if that.

Over and over I scanned his photo, even peering at it

through a magnifying glass and out of those hazel-eyes and determined chin, I'd fashioned a future. My stomach lurched whenever I thought of the moment of impact; my heart fluttered when I envisaged us stepping forward to greet each other, arms outstretched like long-lost lovers as we came together for that first impassioned kiss. I'd raised him up on a pedestal so high I would need an Olympian pole vaulter's prowess to attain the top.

Two days before the date, my instinct led me to ask him some very direct questions. To my surprise, I established that he had not, as I had hoped, been celibate these past three hundred years, but was in fact currently sexually active!! Excuse me??!! You what??!!

When I made some ironic crack like: 'Oh! I'd have thought you'd have been saving yourself...' he replied in his own defence: 'Well, I can't help it if women keep throwing themselves at me.'

This had a very grounding effect, bringing me down to earth with such a bump that I actually considered abandoning the whole project. I was underwhelmed at this piece of news, imagining I held as high a place in his esteem as he had in mine.

And so, with expectations back at sea level, I found myself at his door, and on the threshold of I knew not what...I rang the bell.

The 'My God! You're gorgeous!' greeting gave me back immediate control. Sadly I couldn't reply: 'So are you!' In fact all I wanted to say: 'Shame *you're* not!'

And, in that nanosecond when fantasy meets reality, all hopes of a happy ending – the heart-fluttering anticipation, the weeks of flirty phone calls, emails, conversations, personal revelations and mutual masturbations – faded like a dream at dawn. All a sad and pointless waste of time... As his ship came in, so mine sailed.

My first impression was that he looked nothing like his photo. My second thought was to wonder why his face was all wet. His welcome words were followed by a lunge in my direction to kiss me. I rejected this by raising my hand and saying:

'Sorry I don't do sweaty men!' then immediately regretted it.

Understandably, he looked a bit miffed; he said he'd been working out and had just had a shower. Mollified, I smiled tightly and took in the rest of his appearance: the jeans and bare feet (very nice feet actually) were fine, but the navy nylon gym vest without the requisite musculature was a fashion faux pas if ever I saw one. Considering I'd left my bedroom looking like a cross between *What Not To Wear* and Ms Whiplash's Boudoir, I felt he *could* have made some extra effort.

My second impression was to say: 'Whoops, sorry – my mistake! Bye!' but since we were supposedly 'intimates' I had no option but to follow Andrew into his home. He fussed about pouring me a Scotch and ginger, which he'd bought especially, and opened a jar of almond-stuffed olives which I'd told him I liked. Some effort, then...

My eyes scanned the sparsely-decorated space and noted, with a nod of acceptance, a mega-size box of Durex Featherlights strategically placed within arm's reach on a bookshelf immediately above the deep, tan leather sofa. It conjured up visions of Andrew's naked arse humping up and down as he nailed some poor unsuspecting direct.dater who was *not* going to be me. I sat down opposite the sofa on a leather armchair and looked at him as he prepared the drinks, all the while trying to reconstruct the imaginary boyfriend I'd been 'seeing' for the past six weeks.

Sadly, that man had gone and in his place was an overly tall, underly appealing stranger with a number-one haircut to hide his baldness, for whom I had developed an uncharacteristic affection. Close, but no cigar. Not even a panatela. A smouldering fag-end of a hoped-for love affair, its last flickering ember dying at the bottom of an unwashed ashtray.

It all boiled down to one irreversible truth: sexual chemistry. If it ain't there, there ain't nuttin' you can do about it. Like so many others before and since, I just didn't fancy him.

♀

It was a beautiful evening and we went up onto the roof terrace of his minimal little mews house in Camden Town. It was well planted with a selection of the greenery he'd often been watering during the course of our midnight conversations. I'd asked him once what the noise was.

'Are you pissing?' I'd teased, imagining him talking to me cock in hand, which added a frisson of lewdness to the exchange. Now it was my turn to piss. Pissed off. Pissing in the wind...

Gazing up at the airplanes droning overhead, the clear night sky twinkling with stars, our rendezvous had all the potential of a deeply romantic tryst. Andrew stepped forward at one point and tried to kiss me, but I held my hand up to waylay him muttering: 'No, no, no...' more to myself than to him.

He backed off and I felt rather sorry then; he too had experienced the same eager anticipation. He leaned back dejectedly against the parapet and, by way of apology, I rested gently against him. He wrapped his arms around me and I dropped my head to his shoulder. So close...and yet so far.

My body language was clear. I didn't want to face him but wanted some physical comfort for both our sakes. I felt a sense of loss that it was 'over', sorry at having to reject him, philosophically accepting that, yet again, the journey had been so much more pleasurable than the destination.

He stood very still, breathing against my hair, doubtless picking up my wistful vibes. He did not grow hard nor did I press against him as I would have done had the chemistry been right.

We went back downstairs and, as arranged, he got out his artists' materials and set about painting me. This was a first for me and I found it both intense and relaxing. His own art collection covered the walls and he clearly had some talent. I got comfortable in the chair and watched him closely as he began the watercolour. He pulled funny little moues of concentration and I realised that I was fond of him, but fond did not a passion make. At this point, electricity should have been zig-zagging between us, and he should have thrown down his sketchbook, ripped off his smock and beret, scooped me up in a wild embrace and carried me off to his lair to ravage the pants off me. Instead, we sat in silence for almost an hour, Miles Davis tooting on the stereo. I caught glimpses of the painting at intervals and it was nothing like I'd imagined. I'd fancied a luminous gouache, his appreciation of me reflected onto the sheet in a 'delicate representation of aesthetic beauty'. Instead, he'd done a loud, brash, multi-coloured abstract with green and purple hair and an orange and blue face. Cleverly, you could see it was me in the cheekbone, lip and eye but I didn't want to frame it nor hang it on my wall.

And so the evening brush-stroked to a close. At 11.45 p.m. I said I was tired and got up to leave. He made no objection and came out of the house to walk me to my car. I stood on tiptoe and pecked him out of my life, once on each cheek. He said he'd call.

And so I drove my honed, toned and lace-lingeried body back to my solitary bed. And the drawing board. And a glass of full-fat milk to wash down the very large slice of rich, dark, chocolate cake I'd placed, with malice aforethought, in the fridge earlier...just in case.

MAX
OHM SWEET OHM

It was a warm evening in June and, as usual on a Monday at 6.15 p.m., I change into a pair of exercise pants and set off across the park to do my weekly yoga class. A long stretch, some deep breathing, a gallon of water and a good night's sleep and I'd be ready to face the week ahead and whatever life may throw at me.

Yoga is something I do on a regular basis to keep my body trim, my mind focused and my *prana* rotating in circles of positive *chi*. The teachers alternate so you're never quite sure who you're going to get and this makes it more interesting: one week a gentle Hatha sequence, the next a more dynamic Ashtanga class.

I did, however, have one particular favourite – Max, a single, white male aged around thirty. He was a laidback, hippy-dippy kind of guy with three days' stubble, a Rasta hairdo, Delhi street-market clothing and a 'just-got-back-from-a-year-on-an-Ashram' look about him. With his piercing blue eyes, short, firm frame, and superfit body he was rather engaging even if he did look like he needed a good bath.

Max was an excellent teacher, his lessons enriching in a balanced blend of *asanas* and relaxation which released the tensions and got the good life force coursing through one's body. I always felt deeply energised after these sessions and I left the studio that evening with a lightness of spirit and a spring in my step. Continuing to breathe deeply, I strode purposefully across the park to the shops on Elgin Avenue to buy a few provisions for my fridge.

As I was mulling over the fruit display, Max suddenly appeared at my side. His rucksack was slung casually over his shoulder and his bright, blue eyes were flashing hallo at me.

'Fancy seeing you here,' he says, standing just inside my personal space.

'I live around the corner,' I reply and my flirto-meter starts quivering.

'What are you buying?' he asks.

'Maybe some grapefruit?' I answer. 'Or a watermelon? If it wasn't so heavy for me to carry...'

'I'll carry it for you,' he offers.

'I live in a third floor walk-up,' I warn.

'So by the time I get up there, I'll be needing a slice...' and some sort of fruity foreplay is established.

And so it comes to pass that Max the yoga teacher walks me home and up the stairs carrying all my shopping. I don't understand how this has happened because:

a) I don't fancy him
b) I thought he might be gay

c) I don't make a habit of shagging 'the tennis coach' and

d) I really don't fancy him.

But suddenly there he is, barefoot in my kitchen, and he's opening a bottle of wine, slicing tomatoes for a salad, crumbling feta cheese over the top, unscrewing a jar of pimentos and decorating the end result with kalamata olives and fresh basil. It was surreal. I laid the table, halved an avocado, opened a tin of artichoke hearts, arranged some salami on a platter, stuck a frozen ciabatta in the oven and presto, we had ourselves a sexy little supper.

'Look at the good energy between us,' he comments as we clink glasses.

'I'll light a candle,' I enthuse.

'Light two,' he requests. 'One to keep the other company.'

'Do you know a blessing?' I ask as the candles catch and settle, and he composes himself, closes his eyes, puts his hands together in prayer position and begins to chant an Indian ritual:

'...Ohmmmm...shaanti shaanti shaanti...'

It was all very spiritual and rather beautiful. Despite the fact that it is not Friday night, I counter with the full Jewish *brocha* and then we sit down to eat. The impromptu meal is a like a Mediterranean picnic, creatively cobbled together from the contents of my fridge and store cupboard.

I usually eat alone after yoga watching EastEnders. This was a very welcome change. Max and I toast again, smile contently at each other and talk about travelling, Buddhism, Judaism, our ancestry, and the meaning of life.

After dinner he helps me clear up and we take the candles through to the living-room. I rummage around in a drawer until I find some incense sticks. I knew they'd come in handy sometime and that sometime was now.

'What do you normally do after the class?' I ask as we settle side by side on the sofa.

'I go to a Latin dance club in Shoreditch,' he answers, at which I bound up and put on my Buena Vista Social Club CD.

'We can salsa here,' I say and I drag him up to standing.

He's not very good at it, and when I show off with a backward bend, he nearly drops me, but in fairness, we were a bit tipsy by then. We finish the bottle of wine and he asks if I have anything to smoke.

'If you mean pot – I'm sorry...no...' I answer, but I produce a packet of Cartier Menthol and he accepts one which surprises me as I thought with his ohm-ness 'n all, he'd be ultra-healthy.

So there he is sitting in full lotus position on my couch, in baggy trousers and a frayed old top and he suddenly lunges forward and kisses me. Up to that point, I'd been in some kind of awe of him, respecting his spirituality and endowing him with the mystique of the Orient. I'd believed him to be above other men, on a higher plane, possessed of some visceral inner oneness, detached and untouched by life's temptations. But as our lips meet, along with surprise, I feel a sense of disappointment, and the first thought that comes to me is:

'Oh!... He's only a man.'

I didn't know what I'd been expecting: that he should deny himself carnal knowledge because he was so Zen, wearing a pendant of Krishna's tears on a leather string around his neck? With his Indian aura and sacred leanings, I'd believed him to be a reincarnation of the Dalai Lama, but no, here he is trying to snog and grope me just like any other horny bloke.

(I recently heard that the Dalai Lama carries a mobile phone, albeit in an orange case to match his robe, but even so...!)

Max and I kiss for a while, which is very pleasant, and had I desperately needed a shag, there was one there for the taking. My reticence was principally driven by the thought that, if we went to bed together, it might make it embarrassing for me to go back to his class – if it ended badly or he ignored me or something. So I break the mood and pull him up to dance again. He rises reluctantly, displaying a massive erection angling across the top of his thigh like he'd nicked a prize courgette from the corner shop and shoved it into his trouser pocket. He then asks to see the rest of my flat, which was a barely disguised ploy to get me into the bedroom. I show him round, switching on all the lights as I go and he describes my decor as 'controlled'.

After the tour we return to the kitchen where we hack up the melon, and make a delicious mess tearing off drippy chunks and passing them back and forth to each other from our mouths. It is quite erotic and I can't deny I'm tempted, but I stand my ground and after another hug and kiss, I decide to send him home. He looks dejected and rejected but that is his problem.

Two weeks later, back from a holiday in Spain, I'm getting ready for the Monday yoga class. I feel excited at seeing him again, having mentally decided that tonight is his lucky night. I've done a creative food shop, filling the fridge with lots of little delicacies in the hopes that we can repeat our evening and conclude it in the way that he wanted, which is now what I want too. I spray on a haze of perfume and leave my hair loose and set off across the park. And wouldn't you just know it? Instead of Max we get Sharani. And the following week it's Zara. The week after that I don't go and then, finally, it's Max again.

My heart skips a beat as I enter the studio and there's

plenty of meaningful eye contact during the class. I am totally self-conscious of my every move, the shape of my body during *trikonasana* (the triangle), the invitation of my backside in downward facing dog, the spread of my legs during the inner thigh stretch. The performance pressure is tremendous. I knew it would be. After class I take forever to roll up my mat and put on my trainers until at last everyone else has gone, and it's just Max and I.

'Hi,' I say to him intimately. 'Long time...'

'How are you?' he replies flatly.

'Fine, thanks,' I answer. 'You? Er...are you busy now? Fancy a...meal?'

'A meal?' he asks mockingly. 'Is that what's on offer?'

Cheeky devil, I thought, but I was wrong-footed just the same.

'I am busy actually,' he goes on.

'No problem,' I reply with a mixture of relief and disappointment. 'Maybe some other time...' and I leave the studio and walk home feeling rejected and stupid, much as he must have felt when he left me. We were all square.

The following Monday he is teaching again. I virtually ignore him and concentrate on benefiting from the yoga class. After all, isn't that what I'm here for? But I can't help wondering if he has kept the rest of the evening free in case I ask him over again. But my fridge is empty and in order not to seem like a love-sick fool, I leave the studio with the other pupils and go home alone. I secretly hope he will follow me but he doesn't...

A good few months go past and teachers come and go, then one Monday evening, it's Max again. It's the deep midwinter by now and there are only three of us in the class. I concentrate on my postures, catching his eye from time to time.

'This is the last Monday I'll be teaching,' he announces at the end of the session, 'Ilana will be taking over – she's very good. But if any of you want private lessons or want to get a group together on another evening, I'll give you my mobile number.'

He reads it out and I enter it into my phone. The other two students leave and Max and I are alone again.

'Where are you off to?' I ask casually.

'I'm producing a play,' he answers. 'At the Arts Centre. Actually...' he pauses '...you wouldn't know where I could get some props would you? I need a decanter and some glasses and two identical men's overcoats.'

'I could lend you the decanter and glasses,' I offer immediately. 'As long as I get them back...'

That's another twice I'll have to see you, I thought. God knows why because I really wasn't that into him.

'That'd be great,' he smiles.

'And I know someone in a theatre group,' I continue, remembering my thespy friend. 'They've got a good wardrobe department.'

'Fantastic!' he says. 'I need them for the 25th for four nights.'

'Let me make some enquiries and I'll give you a call. I've got your number now,' and I hold my phone up and wiggle it in the air. I walk back across the dark park feeling bouncy and elated. Hah! I thought. I'll have you yet. As I may have mentioned, I can't bear unfinished business.

I text him the following day and a dialogue goes back and forth to do with the props. I then text him one last question: Too cold for watermelon but fancy a bowl of soup sometime?

The YES flies straight back. Just like that. IN CAPS.
We make a date.

Max comes over later that week and scoffs three bowls of
home-made chicken and vegetable soup like he hasn't eaten
in a month. He breaks the crusty French bread into bite-
size pieces and wipes the bowl with them before handing
it back to me for a refill. He looks like a vagrant, unkempt
and dishevelled, but still there's something endearing about
him. We drink wine and talk and flirt and laugh a lot, and
I love the maternal dichotomy of feeding a young man,
knowing he'll soon become my lover. It fulfils all the earthy
needs in me.

It was a fait accompli that we should go to bed. He was fit,
strong and athletic and we extended the yoga class in a most
inventive way. I was surprised at my own agility (though I
must practise that inner thigh stretch). The first climax was
deep and shuddering and, after we rested, we made love
again. I wish there'd been a camera rolling – our union was
a perfect slow-mo simulation of pages 12–43 of the Kama
Sutra executed with pace and precision. The last words he
said before falling asleep were: 'Hmmm...delicious pussy'.
After that I occasionally texted him: Fancy a bowl of
soup? but we never seemed to be free at the same time
and so the moment passed.

One Monday morning a few months later, Max texted
me to say he would be teaching that night, so we made a
date for him to come over after the class. Being *in flagrante
anticipante*, it was virtually impossible for me to concentrate
on my yoga with a straight face. Every time I caught his
eye, I just wanted to giggle especially as he seemed to have
pitched the lesson personally in my direction. He taught
us some deep breathing exercises designed to give us all 'a

power surge of energy' and kept coming round to adjust our postures, which involved him holding me upside down by the ankles while I was in a shoulder-stand and putting his hands around my waist to increase my backward bend. I'll give you backward bend, I thought...and later that night, I did.

Max came at 8.10 p.m. on that Monday evening and didn't leave until 1.35 p.m. on the Tuesday afternoon having emptied my fridge, wrecked my bed, and sent my sex-ometer off the scale several times. As before, I didn't change the bed. The sheets were stained with chocolate and smelled of sex and him. Why would I change them? I invited Max over twice after that but he declined both times so I stopped asking and then he just disappeared.

I still go to yoga on a Monday and there's a new chap called Leon who teaches us now. He knows my name is Wendy, and he knows I'm fairly bendy. The rest remains to be seen.

ROB-BED
THE ONE THAT GOT AWAY

I should've known better – a woman of my age and experience acting bashful. Waste of precious time if you ask me. You have to *carpe momentum*, never mind *diem*, or it's gone in a flash and never comes again...

It's a Wednesday night and I'm out in the company of my Senior Singles Group. Six men and six women dining in an Italian restaurant in West Hampstead. Combined age? About 720. I'm surrounded by an overweight, opinionated accountant, a balding retired loss adjustor and a diminutive gnome who imports and distributes plastic novelties from the Far East...rock 'n roll it wasn't.

I'm bored out of my brain, on my second glass of Pinot Grigio and scanning the restaurant for a *divertissement*. As if by magic, this appears in the form of a blindingly good-looking if slightly swarthy stranger whose long, muscular legs are straining against the tight fabric of his ripped and faded denim jeans. He is wearing a black linen shirt and his curly, black hair twirls around his face from beneath a baseball cap. I imagine he also has a very hairy chest and body. I do not imagine the cap is there to hide a bald pate.

He is sitting directly across from me in the restaurant with three other guys. Our eyes meet and we share a moment. He leans forward and comments something to his friends who all stare at me, smile and nod to each other. I presume they're not agreeing I look exactly like a 220-pound mud-wrestler. At least that's what the Pinot Grigio is telling me. I stick my chest out a tad, like I've been whistled at by a load of builders. For my part, the evening has taken an interesting turn. My companions are now about as appealing as cold porridge. The next time Cool Dude catches my eye, I flash a smile at him followed by a sultry pout. I can't believe I did that. My daughters would be *so* proud of me!

For the next hour or so, whilst managing to maintain some sort of conversation with Sleepy, Dopey and Grumpy, the dude and I catch each other's eye every seven seconds and the smiles, pouts, blinking and winking continues apace. I lean across to my friend Karina down the table and I tell her what's going on, and that I want to pass him my phone number. This is after two glasses. Imagine if I'd had three...

I write my mobile number on a paper napkin and hand it to her to give to him. Oblivious to the urgency of the matter, she continues eating, drinking and chatting then wipes her mouth on the napkin, screws it up and drops it down onto her empty plate. I shake my head at her but she looks puzzled and shrugs.

Eventually, the evening ends and we allow our ten friends to drizzle away. Karina and I are left alone at the empty table. Dude is standing at the bar chatting to the restaurant owner, throwing the occasional glance in my direction. I fill Karina in on the finer points of my seduction which she takes in then disappears to the ladies room leaving me sitting alone. He now has his back to me and I admire his stature and the firmness of his buttocks in his tight jeans. One day, when I'm old and grey, I'll be arrested for molesting young men at bus stops.

He turns around, sees me sitting alone, raises his eyebrows, takes a couple of steps towards me, hovers in mid-air, loses his bottle and walks back to his table. I'm feigning interest in a wishy-washy watercolour of Florence on the wall above his head. Karina returns from the loo and suggests I now go and that maybe he'll follow me. And then what? A quick grope in the lavvies? No thanks. Not my style at all. I stay put and pretend I've completely lost interest.

His three friends get up and make to leave. He stands up last and looks directly at me in a 'What now?' kind of way. I smile warmly, lift my hand and beckon him over. Blimey. Quel forward! But it had to be done. He approaches our table and in an American accent, which surprises and pleases me, says:

'Hi, I'm Rob.' I was expecting a Stavros.

'Wendy,' I answer grinning triumphantly. 'Take a seat, or do you have to go?'

'No,' he replies, looking round at his friends who are hovering by the door. He winks and waves at them and sits down. They leave the restaurant sniggering.

He's a Canadian on vacation. We start chatting about travel, different climates and what a great place London is. Karina, totally excluded, makes her excuses and leaves. We continue to chit-chat and then hit a lull. He stares very piercingly at me. I stare right back and say the first thing that comes into my head:

'You're a very good-looking boy, you know.'

'Well, thank you,' he answers. 'No one ever said that before.'

'Oh come on,' I act surprised. 'Why do you think I've been looking at you all evening?'

'And why do you think I've been looking at you?'

At that moment, I should have stood up, said 'Come on...' and taken him straight home to bed, but either I lacked the balls or the lady prevailed.

We talk a little longer and then he suggests we take a walk. We leave the restaurant and set off down West End Lane. He makes a point of walking on the kerb side, very well-mannered and properly brought up. The night air is a little chilly and I hug myself and rub my arms to warm up. He unbuttons his linen shirt and drapes it across my shoulders. Aah! Bless. Now in a tight, white t-shirt he is displaying a pair of Superman shoulders and Popeye arms rippling with muscles. I swallow hard.

'So what's a typical tourist day in London?' I ask trying not to drool down my chin. He tells me it always starts with a good workout.

'Well whatever you're doing, it's working!' and I glance appreciatively at him, wondering how cold I have to get before he takes off the t-shirt.

'You look great too,' he responds, looking at me in undisguised admiration.

'Yoga and Pilates,' I reply and we go on to discuss exercise, diet and carb control.

He tells me he's just finished college and is not sure what to do next. When we get to the bottom of the hill by the station, we turn around and walk back up towards my car. The conversation is dragging now and I'm struggling a bit to keep it going. We arrive at my car and I offer him a lift. He declines at first saying he's only staying round the corner but then he says 'OK'.

He opens the car door for me and I get into the driver's seat. I drive the short distance to Frognal and pull over when he tells me to. A hesitant silence ensues during which I woulda coulda shoulda leaned over, taken his divine face in both my hands and planted a sweet and tender kiss on that full, sensuous mouth of his. Instead I sit there like a Mummy waiting to be discovered. I really ought to know by now that younger men love it when an older woman takes the initiative.

'I'll give you my number,' he offers after a short silence. 'Maybe we could meet for coffee?'

And I stupidly answer 'That would be nice. But why don't I give you mine?'

I write my mobile number down on a(nother) scrap of paper and I don't make a note of his. I'm conscious that I should but the moment passes.

'Very nice to meet you,' he says, hesitates for a moment then kisses me on both cheeks. His skin is a little prickly from the day's growth but aah!...so young and firm against mine. And he gets out of the car, gives a little wave and is gone.

Did I hear from him? Did I buffalo...but in fairness, the next day was the day the bombs went off and his parents probably told him to get the hell out of London. If he'd been my kid, I know I would have.

Next time, I'm going to be that sexy older woman he thought I was and make the running. In the restaurant we had it all going on and I should have taken the eager little bull by his eager little horn. Oh, well – at least it proved that at fifty-nine I could still pull a twenty-six-year-old...so gimme a high five for that.

SPRAY IT AGAIN, SAM

I've never really played outside the box. A little light bondage maybe – a coil of black satin rope loosely wrapped around my wrists...a Hermès scarf tightly bound around his eyes while I wriggled and giggled all over the bed as he sought me with his hands and mouth. A tube of Smarties sprinkled across my naked torso for our mutual culinary pleasure. An offer of a certain no-go area to a man I was desperately intent on pleasing. And keeping. (Needless to say once he'd had the best of me, he chucked away the rest of me.)

I'm not into rubber, leather, whips, chains, manacles, studs, pierced nipples, cock rings, handcuffs, straps, spiked wheels, spiked heels, feather dusters or dank cellars with evil accessories hanging from the ceiling. I have no comprehension of a man who stuffs a tangerine in his mouth, places a rope around his neck and beats his meat until he's dead. What's that all about? So imagine my unease when a 34-year-old internet chat mate called Sam kept Instant Messenger-ing me that he would adore to be 'controlled by a superior older woman who would order him around in a rude and arrogant way.' I had had two husbands to do that to, and I got rid of both of them.

He labours this point rather too frequently and keeps sending me those annoying little Smiley winks like I'm meant to know exactly what he's talking about. Every time I get bored and write 'Must go now – got ironing to do' or some such dousing comment, he immediately offers to come round and do it for me. It's tempting, I must say. He also wants to tidy up my knicker drawer. With his teeth. Yeah – well – whatever...

The whole thing makes me feel rather uncomfortable, but I'm also slightly curious. And it's not *really* a problem: I could do dominatrix with my eyes closed and my hands tied behind my back. I could also see myself strutting around my flat in PVC thigh boots and a riding crop while some poor bugger licks my skirting boards. People get paid a lot of money for that sort of thing and it would save Maria the trouble so she could get on with polishing the silver properly for a change. The idea also appeals of getting him round one day when I'm feeling particularly crabby, and giving him what for. He would embody all the men who've ever dissed me. It would be better than counselling or even a boxercise class. Anyway, Sam is clearly gagging to meet me and, in the spirit of a good wind-up, I play along. We also have some fairly grown-up conversations and he sounds like a decent and good person. He loves his mum, has a disabled sister he often takes care of and, at weekends, he plays in a pub band. But he has this dark side which I want to explore so eventually we make a date.

I walk round to the local wine bar and stand in a doorway

directly across the road. I'm a bit early but there's a young man who fits Sam's description (only shorter and fatter) pacing about outside. He is looking this way and that and keeps checking his mobile.

I emerge from my *cachette* and stride across the road in a way that makes him notice me. He looks incredibly flustered and stuffs his phone back in top pocket. He draws himself up to his full height (liar) and smiles nervously. I shake hands with him which affirms my role as Arthur and his as Martha.

We enter the wine bar, and I sit down and ask for a Bloody Mary. I play the part of being domineering and abrupt, which is out of character as I'm normally all girly and gracious when I meet a man for the first time. He flushes to the tips of his mousy pink eyelashes and scuttles off like a junior butler on his first day at Buck House. While he's at the bar, I appraise him critically from where I sit: curly fair hair, round face, piggy nose, baby soft mouth and a chin which will become several in the fullness of time. I imagine him in a big nappy and a knitted bonnet all squashed up in a Silver Cross pram. I'm going to need more than one Bloody Mary to play this game.

He returns to the table and spills some of the drinks as he sits down. I glare at him and tut, then mop up the drips with a napkin. He smiles nervously, unsure if I am really cross or just faking. I feel terrible as I would never normally be this cruel, but I'm in character and that's what he wants. We begin a rather stilted conversation which loosens up as the alcohol takes charge. I keep to safe subjects while I appraise the situation and, eventually, go to the bar and buy a second round. Sometimes I ask myself what the hell I'm doing with my life...

As always in these situations, the telephonic titillation

and email innuendo is less powerful once you're face to face. By the end of my second drink, however, he is becoming marginally more attractive. I am turned on by the empowering feeling of being completely in control of him. I want to explore this further. He is a sweet boy with a tremendous complex shared by the majority of the male population. I'm sure Cynthia Payne would have plenty to say about this, having entertained the great and the good in the form of High Court judges, doctors and respected politicians (is that an oxymoron?) who all craved being used and abused whilst wearing romper suits and sucking a dummy. Mothers obviously have a lot to answer for and the modern use of the word 'motherfucker' could only happen in a culture where the force of family is a fast-dying myth.

As I feel perfectly safe with him, I suggest we walk the short distance to my home. We leave the wine bar and I notice he has become quite rosy. I am feeling rather rosy too, and decide to get deeper into the game we are playing. I give him a withering look and stride on ahead. He trots behind me.

'Come along now!' I command in my best governess voice, and he gives the appearance of trying to keep up. We reach my front door and I usher him in. He stands in the hallway looking around and, from God knows where, I point towards the bathroom and say:

'You. Undressed. In the shower. Now. And leave the door open.'

His eyes flash between terror and delight and I turn him around and give him a little push. He pads off down the corridor. I wait a couple of minutes and then I follow. He is standing in the middle of the bathroom in his boxer shorts and socks awaiting further instruction. His body isn't bad, though he could lose a few pounds and tone up a bit, but he's young, keen and at a distinct disadvantage.

'Turn around!' I command and I pull down his shorts and smack him quite hard on his behind. He sucks his breath in sharply and I feel a surge of electric energy. I am getting really horny and I can't believe I'm doing this, let alone enjoying it.

'Nanny is going to wash you now,' I say tersely, making it up as I go along, 'because you're a dirty little boy, aren't you?'

He nods enthusiastically and I point for him to pull his pants down and take his socks off. He has a lazy lob. It bobs forth then settles on the left and, in its semi-flaccid state, it shows enormous promise. I push him into the shower and turn the water on.

'Wash!' I order and he squeezes some shower gel into the palm of his hand and soaps his body all over, never taking his eyes off me for an instant. When he goes to rub his genitals I smack his hand away and reach down to do it for him. I slide my soapy hand back and forth along his shaft, and he rises to full erection. He is glowing from head to toe like all his birthdays have come at once. I am wet in more ways than one.

'Who's a very bad boy indeed?' I ask somewhat rhetorically.

'Me, Nanny!' he answers enthusiastically, like a school boy who knows the right answer to a particularly taxing question. 'You make me *so very* bad!'

'And what happens to bad boys, eh?' I request, my starched uniform positively stiffening as I speak.

'They have to be punished?' he pleads hopefully.

'Yes,' I affirm. 'Severely punished! This behaviour will not do at all! Come out at once!'

I turn the shower off and throw him a towel and he starts to dry himself.

'Shorts on only!' I command, with absolutely no idea

what to do next. I go into the kitchen and pour myself a large vodka and tonic, then make one for him. I return to the bathroom.

'You have to drink this nasty medicine,' I say, handing him the glass. 'To make you behave better and not make Nanny so cross. And then...' taking a slug of my own drink which gives me time to think '...when Nanny calls you, you have to come into the nursery and show me how very sorry you are.'

I turn away and go into my bedroom where I take off my trousers and top. Underneath, I am wearing a black satin lace-up basque with suspenders, black seamed stockings and knee-length black leather boots.

'Samuel?' I shout very angrily. 'Nursery. Now!'

He runs down the corridor and into my room. I am standing with my legs apart and my hands on my hips. He screeches to a halt and his eyes open wide, then shut, then open again like a blinking doll.

'Down!' I bark at him and he drops to his knees.

I open a drawer and remove the dog-lead I have purchased specially for the occasion and I attach it loosely around his neck. He is practically wimpering now. I pat him on the head to calm him and he turns his face up to mine. He sticks out his tongue and pants like a puppy.

'Good boy,' I say, trying not to laugh. 'Walkies!'

And I lead him up and down the corridor a few times swaying my hips as I go. He crawls behind me on his hands and knees and once or twice I yank the lead.

'Heel!' I command not quite sure when he stopped being a boy and turned into a dog.

'Now...' I say once we are back in the bedroom. '...Nanny needs some help with something.'

I get my shoe-cleaning kit from the cupboard and hand it to him. I stick the pointy toe of my black leather boot in his face and he begins to polish it lovingly, paying extra attention to the heel which I grind around in his hand. As I look down at him I can see the shiny, bulbous head of his fully erect penis poking through the slit in his boxer shorts.

'Oh!' I say in mock anger. 'What on earth is that?!'

And he stops polishing and fumbles around trying to tuck it away out of sight.

'Stand up, you wicked boy!' I order and he gets to his feet hanging his head in shame.

'Now show Nanny exactly what you've got in your pants!'

He rummages around inside his fly and presents me with a magnificently long, straight, strawberry-pink phallus.

'And what do you call *that*?' I ask sitting down on the edge of my bed with my legs apart.

'That's a lovely present for Nanny to play with,' he says proudly and takes a couple of steps towards me.

I consider my options, take a long pull on my drink and bend my head towards the extended lolly. I wrap my lips around it and bring the ice cube forward in my mouth so it melts against his skin. He gasps and his knees buckle slightly as he pushes deeper into my mouth. I suckle it for a while then bite it gently all around the rim and withdraw.

It all went rather fast after that. I lay back on the bed, hook my finger inside the crotch of my basque and pull it aside. He climbs aboard and I push his head down and hold it fast.

'Be nice to Nanny, you vile boy...' I murmur – and he licks efficiently, guided by my gyrations.

When I've finished, I pull his boxers off and roll him over onto his stomach. I straddle him and spank him lightly on both buttocks grinding myself against his flesh until I'm almost ready to come again. Then I turn him back over, sit on him and ride him as hard as I can.

'You wait until I tell you!' I order and, to his credit, he holds on until I climax one more time. I climb off him and collapse on my back more than satisfied. I suggest he might like to finish himself off between my breasts, bleating all the while what a disgusting thing he's doing, and how I shall have to think up a more severe punishment for him next time.

There wasn't to be a next time, but in my mind, at that moment, I could hardly wait...

ORLANDO
MAN OVERBORED

It was a chilly Sunday morning in late March. The phone rang.

'What are you doing next Christmas?' asks Lydia in that way she has of lunging in without even a 'Hallo, how are you?'

'No idea. Why?'

'I've just been offered a villa in Antigua. £75.00 a night!'

I do hate having to make such difficult decisions: dry turkey with boiled Brussels in bleak old Blighty or Coconut Shrimp with Mango on a white sandy beach in the Caribbean. Hmmm...let me see...

I did a quick head count. All my nearest and dearest would be somewhere else.

'Sounds good to me!' I reply and without further ado we click our respective 'Book Now' buttons and nine months later, we're stepping off a jumbo jet onto the sweltering tropical tarmac of our very own island in the sun. It was Christmas Day and the weather report read: Gatwick 4°, Antigua 28°. What a result! Rather like Arsenal playing the Barbuda Boys Second XI.

Actually getting out of the airport was another matter. The terminal is a crumbling Third World prefab with no air conditioning and queues of hot, sweaty, jet-lagged tourists fanning themselves with their passports as they inch forward towards the petty bureaucracy that is Immigration. It took us 1½ hours to get our papers stamped, which makes you irritable after a nine-hour flight. It was not exactly 'Welcome to Antigua' – more like: 'Wha' choo people doin' heeah?' What do they think we're doing? Trying to steal their sunshine? Import and distribute illegal substances? The local radio station is probably called Spliff FM and the air is so full of weed, mon, they may as well rename the place Ganja Heights!

We finally clear customs and, after a bumpy cab ride over potholed roads, we arrive at our villa in Jolly Harbour in the late afternoon. Bags are dumped, bedrooms selected and before you could say Rum Punch, all stress was forgotten as we clink glasses on that white sandy beach while the sun sets spectacularly into the azure waters of the Caribbean...

(Flashback to London: Great Uncle Albert is snoring in front of the TV. The top three inches of his flies are undone. He's watching the umpteenth rerun of a Morecambe and Wise Christmas Special as he chuffs silently into the beige dralon fabric of his fireside chair.) Quick! Return to Paradise!

♀

My friend Lydia had recently been the victim of a familiar form of torment by a wealthy playboy who was no better than he ought to be. They'd dated in the loosest sense
of the word for four months and all she'd got out of it was
one night in a posh hotel (he was there on business anyway) with champagne, candles and Charbonnel &
Walker chocolates all provided by her. Being a giving
kinda gal, she then invited him to her home for endless
lunches and dinners and never got taken out again. He
was a tight bastard and Lydia eventually acknowledged
that the relationship, such as it was, was going to hell in
a handcart. Unlike the red-blooded Action Man he
purported to be, she soon discovered he had Ribena
in his veins when he cancelled a Thursday night date on
the Monday saying he thought he 'had a cold coming
on'. What a wuss! She also admitted that he was crap in bed.

'There's more action on a mortuary slab than having sex
with him!' she complained. Our kid's from Middlesbrough
and she doesn't sugar coat it.

Veering between dumping him in a good way and
dumping him in a bad way, we decided on the latter.
Many an entertaining hour was then spent composing
'You're dumped' texts, which is very liberating especially
when it's happening to someone else. The words 'and
another thing...' kept cropping up as she recalled more
and more ways in which he'd dissed her, primarily by
never inviting her to his home, let alone his bed; his
excuse was that he wanted to 'change the mattress' after
his ex-wife had left (subtext: I've had various other
women in and out and their stuff is still all over the
place).

So for Lydia the holiday was a mission to find a new man
for the New Year and purge herself of the old one. I wasn't
bothered. I was just happy to have got away after a fairly

hyper few months at work.

Despite the friendly, laid-back ambience of Jolly Beach and its glorious surroundings, Lydia spent the first two days staring miserably into the middle distance re-reading the In and Out boxes on her mobile phone. She also read a book entitled *It's Called a Break-up because it's Broken,* a relationship manual for the Hard of Accepting and those of us who can't quite face the bleeding obvious...

On our second night in Antigua, we'd arranged to meet some friends from England who'd just sailed their yacht over from the Azores (as you do if you've got a yacht and the navigational skills to find the Azores from Portsmouth in the first place). And for me, at this juncture, the holiday took a delightful turn.

We were sitting with Mr & Mrs Yacht Owners and their friends at Skulduggery Bar in Falmouth Harbour drinking Kaffeine Kickers (a lethal mix of double espresso, crème de cacao, white rum and paint stripper) when two young studs ambled up and sat down to join us. My endorphins leapt like dolphins in an aqua show as they were introduced as 'the crew' – a pair of tall, tanned dudes who'd just sailed a 60-footer across the Atlantic – and if that's not a macho turn-on, then please tell me what is. One of them was Canadian, his body a testament to the artistry of his tattooist; the other one was Australian and the words that came to mind were: 'have him washed and brought to my tent.' He had something of Orlando Bloom about him – a Pirate of the Caribbean who could plunder my vessel any time he wanted. Ooh! I thought excitedly. Now I too have A Mission...and I latched on to him like a well-oiled gate.

It's not difficult to command a man's attention, no matter his or your age – you just need to know which buttons to press.

Button One: make positive eye contact.

Button Two: smile warmly and invitingly in his direction.

Button Three: ask him some pertinent questions about himself.

I don't know if he knew he was being gently hit on, but with very little effort, he slid into my frying pan like a fresh egg into hot butter.

Orlando regaled me with seafaring yarns of the 22-day Atlantic crossing: the eerie solitude of the night watch, the awesome shooting stars jetting across the black sky, the whales who came to play alongside showing their white bellies as they dived beneath the prow, the unpredictable wind changes, the migrating birds who hitched a ride on the rail, the giant marlin they hooked and then put back – I hung fascinated on his every word. There was an untainted innocence about him overlying something subtly smouldering. He was like a gangly calf that would grow into a fighting bull, or a quiet mountain that didn't know it was really a volcano.

I asked Orlando what he missed most when he was at sea expecting him to answer 'sex', but he said 'fresh vegetables' which was very Zen and rather sweet. We discovered we shared the same favourite midnight snack: toast with peanut butter, mashed banana and honey. We decided the world lacked chocolate-covered Pringles and I promised to make them for him if we ever got into a kitchen together. He told me about his passion for surfing and how he'd been dumped by various girlfriends for always being late when surf was up. I told him about my passion for antique hunting and the adrenalin charge of a successful auction bid. Lydia and the others became a blur on the edges of my consciousness as I focused my attention solely on this boy. From time to time, she caught my eye and I flicked her a wink.

As Orlando and I talked, we bonded, and our looks began exchanging different messages to those of our lips. In terms of eye-candy, he was the mutt's nuts: sea-green eyes, good straight nose, sexy little mouth, five-day stubble, a well-muscled and deeply bronzed body, but his crowning glory was his shoulder-length hair – a tousled mane of dark curls tied back in a ponytail out of which escaped sun-bleached coils which framed the edges of his youthful face. I wanted to reach out and twist the tendrils round my finger. I wanted to reach out and wrap the body in my arms...

Later in the evening, we all went out for dinner and continued our connection while we shared our food. I'd ordered vegetarian 'cos he did and when the meal was over and it was time to part, I stood on tiptoe to kiss him goodnight. He seemed a little surprised at this. Despite our growing closeness, he may have felt an element of 'us and them', him being crew and me being a guest of his bosses 'n all, not to mention a different generation. But I didn't care. He smelt as fresh and wild as the sea and, like the marlin, I was hooked.

♀

The following day Lydia and I were basking on our sun beds, me deep in Orlando, when a text came through from one of our friends on the yacht.

Sailing into Driftwood Bay. Join us for lunch?

I yelped with delight and dashed to the beach bar loo to do what I could with my hair and face. Before too long, the yacht hove into view. I paced the shore impatiently as they faddled around dropping anchor then they all climbed aboard the tender (Love me tender?

Tender is the night?) and were soon speeding through the swell towards us. I could see my boy sitting on the back steering, his hair blowing in the wind, and a surge of excitement and anticipation coursed through me. We settled at a big, round table for lunch and managed once again to sit side by side. Whenever our eyes met we shared a secret smile.

In the afternoon the boys went off get fuel and provisions and, as the day turned to dusk, we swapped our fruit punches for rum punches, and began to make plans for the evening. Lydia and I went back to the villa to shower and change and when we returned to the bar two new men had joined the group. One was a middle-aged yachtsman who fitted all of Lydia's criteria; the other was a young American guy who was already known to the rest of our crew.

As luck would have it, I managed to get the dream team down my end of the table. They were talking travel plans when the sailing was through, and Orlando said he was thinking of coming to London. As I had my little laptop with me, I offered to go online and check the price of flights for him. He pulled his chair up close to mine and peered over my shoulder as I typed. I looked down at his slim, brown feet in their rubber flip flops and I wanted to stroke my toes across them.

There were no free networks within range, so I paid $10.95 to link to a WiFi server and I put the charge on my credit card.

'You're going to owe me for this you know,' I teased, wondering how he'd rise to that challenge.

'Oh...' he replied naively. 'Er...OK...' and he reached for his wallet.

I laughed at his naivety and pushed the wallet away.

'Don't worry about the money!' I said teasingly. 'I'll

collect the debt some other way...' and then, may his dear sweet mother forgive me, I eye-fucked the hell out of him.

Contrary to popular belief, this sort of behaviour doesn't come that naturally to me. I still like a man to chase me until I catch him but the rum punches were doing their evil work and, for obvious reasons, I was living in the moment.

As the evening wore on, Lydia disappeared off with her millionaire to drink champagne and dance the night away on some distant beach. Mr & Mrs Yacht Owners and the other 'grown-ups' headed off to the Yacht Club – an invitation which I politely declined – and by a mixture of fate and design, I was left alone with the three young guys. My head was reeling. I couldn't believe my luck. We moved on to another bar and I used the opportunity to do some research. I bought them a round of drinks which drew them closer to me and steered the conversation to my favourite topic: relationships.

'So how do you guys cope with all the travelling?' I asked, sipping on another brightly-coloured cocktail. 'Keeping in touch with girlfriends must be a nightmare, no?'

They sniggered and looked knowingly at each other and I knew I'd struck a chord. The American, who at thirty-two was the eldest, volunteered some vital information.

'I keep it simple,' he said. 'No ties, no lies. And what goes on tour stays on tour... Actually,' he added, looking pointedly at me, 'my last girlfriend was an older woman...'

'Really!?' I said with pleasure. 'I can't say I'm surprised. It's a growing trend, you know. Since most same age marriages end in divorce, we have to explore the alternatives. I think over 60 per cent of current liaisons are between couples where the female is older. And what about the rest of you? Any Mrs Robinsons in your repertoires?!'

'I have!' boasted the Canadian enthusiastically. 'I dated an older woman for a while. I was twenty-six and she was thirty-eight, and it was great while it lasted. But she always wanted to pay for everything and that undermined me.'

I took note.

'Older women make better company,' added the American. 'They're so much more interesting...and experienced...they know a lot of tricks!'

And we all laughed. I'd heard this one before and it never failed to amuse me.

'And we don't like the word "toyboy"!' Orlando cut in. 'It makes us sound like you just want to use us and throw us away.'

'Like men have been doing with women since the beginning of time?' I asked sardonically. 'We're only redressing the balance. My last relationship was with a much younger man...and that worked for a long time...'

'There's definitely a strong attraction from our side,' commented the Canadian. 'How does it work from yours? Apart from the obvious?'

'Well "the obvious" is the main event in any relationship to begin with,' I said. 'Later you compromise. Find new stuff to do together. Communicate and don't let it get stale. And be aware that it probably won't last...'

I looked around the bar. A couple of overweight, balding, middle-aged men were sitting at a nearby table nursing their drinks. They were hardly noteworthy, one overweight, balding, middle-aged man being much like another. I used them to illustrate my point.

'The reason so many older women are with younger men is sitting right there. Look at those two,' I nodded in their direction. 'Although they're my generation, I feel totally disconnected from them. They've let themselves go which is really unappealing. I know loads of attractive, sexy, vibrant older women but the men...eeuw! They think they can pull you because they've got money and a pulse and that any single woman is desperate for a man at any cost. Personally, I'd rather eat pizza with you lot than caviar with any of them.'

'You are so cool and sophisticated,' enthused the American. 'How old are you?'

I froze on the spot. He'd asked the Forbidden Question. I pursed my lips at him.

'You never ask a lady...'

'I'd guess around forty-six?' cut in the Canadian.

'Forty-eight?' queried Orlando.

'Maybe...fifty-two?' hesitated the more mature American. He was on very dangerous ground.

I laughed in a cavalier fashion and shook my head.

'You'll never know! Anyway, what does it matter? We're sharing our stories and enjoying each other's company. What difference do the numbers make? Your energy...it's inspiring and it rubs off on me...'

'And we're getting great energy off you too!'

'So my age doesn't matter. Right?'

And as they nodded Frank Sinatra crooned in my head: *When I was fifty-nine...it was a very good year...*

The conversation moved on to other topics: art, music, places they'd been, cities they'd seen. They were all quite worldly and well-travelled. I moved a little closer to Orlando, leaning lightly towards him so the bare skin of my arm brushed against his. I wanted to let him know that out of the three, he was definitely my favourite.

Some nights Venus and Mars align in perfect symmetry and when they do, wonderments can happen. Just as I was pondering how the evening might end, Lydia rang me on my mobile to ask if I minded her staying overnight with her new 'friend'.

'We're on the other side of the island,' she shouted tipsily. 'Will you get a cab and come and join us? He's got an amazing villa with LOADS of bedrooms – you and I can share...I'm not going to sleep with him...'

She giggled hysterically and I heard a slap as she whispered: 'Gerroff!'

'I'm staying put, thanks!' I answered. 'I've got my own fish to fry. You have fun and call me in the morning. Good luck!'

Shortly after, the Yacht Owners came into the bar to say they were heading back to the boat and what did the boys want to do. Apocalypso was moored out in the harbour and once the tender went back to her, that was where it would stay. The boys looked at each other and hesitated, then inspiration hit me like a bolt of lightning.

'They can stay with me!' I exclaimed. 'Lydia's sleeping out, so there's plenty of room at the villa. I don't mind putting the boys up for the night. They can come back in the morning...it'll be safer anyway...we've all had a bit to drink!'

I caught the briefest flash of a look between Orlando and the Canadian and another piece of the jigsaw slotted neatly into place.

We moved on to the Karaoke Bar at the Casino and took the piss out of the singers for a while, and then wandered back along the marina towards the villa complex. It was about 1.30 a.m. by then and the Canadian stopped at a callbox to phone his girlfriend back home. Orlando and I moved away to give him some space and I took the chance to share my thoughts with him.

'I'm not sure what to do about the sleeping arrangements...' I confessed, trying to gauge where he was at with all this. I had rather taken command of the night. I looked up into his sea-green eyes and stood as close to him as I dared.

'There's a sofa bed, a twin room and a double.' I explained. 'Where would you like to sleep?'

He emitted a nervous laughter like he'd be thrown to the crocodiles if he got it wrong.

'Let's see when we get back?' he replied in that Australian lilt, which bought us both a little time. In the circumstances that was probably the correct answer.

As I moved away, I noticed the shape at the front of his cut-off jeans had altered dramatically.

The Canadian's phone card ran out halfway through his conversation, and he slammed the phone angrily against the box before hanging it up. He'd obviously been in the middle of something crucial and was fuming and muttering as he stomped straight past us.

'I will *never* get to that place with her again...' he moaned despairingly. 'Fucking stupid...'

I caught up with him and touched his arm sympathetically.

'Anything I can do?' I offered. 'Do you want to talk about it?'

He shook his head and walked on, moody and withdrawn. I left him to it and dropped back to join the others. As soon as we reached the villa, he flopped face down onto the sofa and covered his head with his hands. Before long, he fell asleep, snoring softly.

One down, two to go, I thought.

The American was hovering and I knew that the next move was up to me.

'Come on Mike,' I said, gesturing towards the staircase. 'I'll show you where *you're* going to sleep'.

I shot a quick look at Orlando which said: Stay right where you are and await further instructions.

I took the American up to the twin room which I'd been occupying and pointed to the bed which hadn't been slept in.

'Help yourself to whatever you want,' I said, indicating the ensuite bathroom. 'There's a towel on the rail you can use. Sleep well. See you in the morning.' And I blew him a quick kiss and closed the door firmly behind me.

I went slowly back downstairs. Orlando was riveted to the spot exactly where I'd left him. I crooked my finger and beckoned him towards me and the words of a long-forgotten rhyme came to my mind:

'Will you come into my parlour!' said the Spider to the Fly
'Tis the prettiest little parlour that you ever will spy!'
'Oh no, no' said the little Fly, 'I've often heard it said
They never, ever wake again who sleep upon your bed!'

As he approached me, I turned slowly and headed back upstairs towards the double room. He followed me like a lamb to the slaughter. I stood aside to let him go in and I closed and locked the door behind us.

Once we were alone together, I suddenly felt very sober and rather uncomfortable. I sat down on the edge of the bed.

'I feel like I've kidnapped you,' I confessed, running my fingers through my hair.

He raised his arm behind his back as if being held in an arm lock.

'Yeah, right,' he said, but somehow I wasn't convinced.

'Would you like to take a shower?' I suggested and he nodded and disappeared into the bathroom.

♀

I stayed sitting on the edge of the bed wondering what the hell to do next. I had cunningly inveigled a 25-year-old into my boudoir but bizarrely, instead of elated I felt guilty. Now we were alone together, the intimacy we'd been building had been replaced by a certain awkwardness. All I'd wanted was to be alone with him but I'd made that decision for both of us leaving him no choice. To hell with it, I thought, dismissing my conscience. You're in the water now. You may as well swim.

I took my clothes off but not my underwear and I got into bed. While Orlando was showering, I arranged myself in a variety of contrived postures none of which felt natural, attractive or remotely sexy. When the door opened and he came out wearing nothing but a white towel around his waist (oh God...) I was feeling anything but cool and sophisticated.

Orlando crossed wordlessly to the other side of the bed and dropped the towel as he turned to get in. Just before switching off the light which plunged the room into total darkness, I caught sight of the most beautiful firm, creamy, white buttocks I had ever seen, contrasting starkly with his deep mahogany back and legs. My self-confidence was deserting me and I lay there stiffly waiting for him to make the first move.

'Do you normally climb into bed with total strangers?'

Orlando's accusing voice broke the silence between us.

'You're *not* a stranger,' I protested defensively. I had, after all, known him for two whole days.

'I am,' he argued and swung himself on top of me.

We kissed clumsily and writhed around a bit. There was no passion or magic and I wasn't remotely turned on. Orlando seemed hell bent on getting the whole thing over with as quickly as possible. He dry humped me briefly until he achieved a semi-erection at which point I decided *I'd* better put on a bit of a show. I rolled him onto his back and guided his hands to take my bra off. He fumbled with it and eventually got it unhooked, but expressed no interest in my breasts once they were released to him. I slid down slowly towards his cockpit nibbling and kissing as I went, but by the time I got there, nothing whatsoever awaited me. I lingered there awhile doing the necessary, but to no avail. He must have been embarrassed as he twisted me back beneath him, pulled my pants off, pumped against me a few more times until he was hard, entered me, thrust once or twice, and came. Or pretended to. It was the most unsatisfactory sex I'd ever had. And the quickest. My body had been neither engaged nor appreciated and as for my mind, let's not even go there.

He rolled off me and surprised me by kneeling between my parted legs. He seemed to be doing things arse upwards. Foreplay became afterplay as he lifted both my feet in his hands and began to massage them which felt intimate and very nice. He stroked lightly up and down my legs, reaching the top then stroking back down again. I raised my hips to invite him but he did not do as I had hoped. After a short while, sensing his heart was hardly in it, I stopped his hands with mine.

'It's late, baby,' I whispered. 'You must be very tired...'

'Yes. I am,' he answered softly.

I pulled him down next to me and we had our best moment then as he held me tightly in his arms. I lay my head upon his chest and did what I'd wanted to do since we'd met. I stroked his long, dark, curly hair and imprinted his firm, young body against mine. That was more visceral than when I'd had him inside me, but still I felt empty, shallow and disappointed. I knew the meaning of regret at that moment, knowing that what I'd done, and the way that I'd done it, had been wrong. I'd taken an innocent friendship, something pure and unsullied, and I'd corrupted it.

Orlando fell asleep and soon, when we got hot and sweaty and stuck together, he moved away from me. I lay awake until the first light of dawn suffused the room and I watched him lovingly, longingly, the weight of conscience heavy in my heart. I longed to turn the clock back to when nothing beat between us but the delicious pulse of possibility.

Reality sucks, and I'd failed to remember that sugared almonds taste so much better savoured... NOT smashed to smithereens with a sledgehammer.

♀

At around 6.30 a.m. I began to get curdling cramps in the pit of my stomach. They rumbled and grumbled like a witch's cauldron and I lay there in agony fearing the worst. Tom used to call me 'Tupperware', so convinced was he that my bottom had a vacuum seal, but that morning, as fate would have it, I was as windy as Chicago. The pains came over me like the contractions of childbirth and I clenched my sphincter as tight as I could praying nothing evil would escape me. Orlando's eyes were closed but he had stirred once or twice and the room was now filled with the cruel mockery of morning. I was dying for the loo but couldn't trust myself to move, let alone cross the room and have my arse explode only yards away from where my boy lay sleeping. After what seemed like an eternity listening to my stomach phftt-phftt like a percolator, I lost the fight. The beastly bubbles burst from between my clenched buttocks and broke free from my front bottom in a series of chuffing little fanny farts which split the silence like a mortar in a mortuary. My mortification knew no bounds. Please God, I prayed, just take me now...

I got up quickly, wriggled into Lydia's towelling robe and rushed from the room and down the stairs to the guest loo where I dispersed the dregs of my dignity down the toilet. If the sleeping Canadian heard me, so be it. I'd sunk about as low as I could go...

I had a whore's bath and cleaned away the smudges of last night's make up, then crept back upstairs praying Orlando would still be in the land of nod. To my dismay he was up, standing by the window with his shorts on and his t-shirt in his hand.

I was too embarrassed to look him. I lowered my head and crossed the room to hide my face against his chest: an apology, an acknowledgement, a reaching out, a way of hiding my shame and humiliation. He held me because he had to and then we parted. I went back downstairs and put the kettle on. The others were up and we greeted each other politely like the strangers that we were.

Damn reality and the cold light of day...give me the night and the madness...

I made coffee and prepared a fruit platter, retreating into the kitchen comfort of slicing bananas and melon neatly onto a plate. Orlando came downstairs and went straight out onto the deck. The Canadian got off the couch and joined him and they stood talking awhile. No smiles were exchanged. No laughter passed their lips.

They ate their breakfast, thanked me for my hospitality and left. I expected at least a peck from Orlando...but nothing. I forced a bright smile and a breezy 'Take care, guys!' and I shut the door behind them. I then began the penitential task of beating myself up. I felt like a slag. I'd acted like a slag. Maybe deep down in my mortal soul, I really was a slag.

I cleaned the kitchen with Vim and vigour (industry cures melancholy) then had a boiling hot shower in the hopes my sins and I would dissolve down the drain and never be heard of again. Mercifully, Lydia arrived home shortly after and we fell upon each other like long-lost sisters.

'I shagged him!' she whimpered, her face a picture of revulsion and disgust.

'So did I!' I groaned and we clung together in a muddle of self-reproach and semi-hysterical simulated sobbing. After a lengthy post-mortem on the night's events, we forgave ourselves and each other, put on swimsuits and walked down to the beach bar for breakfast. I hadn't reckoned on the bloody yacht still being in the bay and I had to sit with my back to it, muttering: 'For fuck's sake! This is doing my head in.'

We ordered poached eggs on toast, mango juice and coffee and every so often I asked Lydia to update me on the shipping forecast. The yacht continued to bob blamelessly on the clear, calm waters as if all was well with the world.

Lydia's need to discuss her future broke through my stream of consciousness as she regaled me with the details of her night of lurve. In the inebriated magic of the moonlight, the millionaire had appeared to be the answer to a maiden's prayer. He seemed utterly enamoured of her and talked of whisking her off to Aspen at the earliest opportunity. Listening dreamily to his pre-coital promises, she'd fantasised him into a tall, dark, handsome Sugar Daddy who would lift the weight of work and single motherhood off her shoulders and give her the life she aspired to. She wept with emotion when she told me he'd even offered to put her boys through private school – it was all she'd ever dreamt of and she couldn't believe her luck.

However, in the harsh light of morning, he'd materialised from beneath the duvet as the living incarnation of E.T. To add to her confusion, he'd then proposed, offering to 'sprinkle moon dust in her hair of gold and starlight in her eyes of blue.' Her battle to convince herself she could overlook certain unmistakeable facts failed miserably as we weighed up the pros and cons:

Pro: five-star lifestyle with all the trimmings to be lived in the company of...

Con: a shrivelled, brown alien with a flat head and no shoulders.

He'd said he was sixty but as we deconstructed him, like time itself, he grew older and older, until by midday he was practically prehistoric, at which point the argument collapsed and so did we.

♀

We were just about to go for a brain-cleansing power walk along the beach followed by a long swim, when a text suddenly came through from you-know-where.

Sailing back to English Harbour. Want to come?

Lydia and I stared at each other. A look of desperate longing crossed my face. A chance to make amends? I nodded urgently.

`Great idea!` she texted back. `Where shall we meet and when?`

`Your mooring. 45 mins` came the reply.

And so I lived to love another day. We dashed back home for make-up and a change of clothing, and not long after saying goodbye with a rock in my heart, I was saying hallo again like the night had never happened. Denial is a wondrous thing...

♀

Needless to say, the dynamic between us was completely different. No eye contact was made as I climbed aboard the tender which he proceeded to drive out of the marina like a powerboat racer set on winning the Grand Prix. We reached the yacht, hauled ourselves aboard, raised the anchor and headed south. This time it was definitely 'us and them'.

As the skipper sailed the boat out through the coastal shallows, I approached Orlando while he knelt scrubbing away at an oil spill on the bleached teak deck. I didn't want to follow him around like a lovesick puppy but I needed some reassurance that he didn't find me repulsive and detestable. I managed to engineer a conversation about yacht maintenance which he answered politely, but the spark between us had definitely gone. I could have offered him a month's holiday in Hawaii with a selection of the latest Salomon surfboards, but he clearly no longer fancied me. He finished his scrubbing and went below and I skulked off to the seating area to try and enjoy the day's sail.

To give us our money's worth Mr Yacht Owner decided to go the long way round, and instead of *The Blue*

Lagoon, the voyage suddenly turned into *The Cruel Sea*. We were set fast on a course towards Guadeloupe and the ocean soon became dark, rough and menacing. The yacht was a slick racing vessel and, at a speed of some 14 knots, she tilted sharply. Us land-lubbers had to hang on for grim death lest we be swept overboard and lost. Lydia was turning green and occasionally clutched her stomach as she shot me an 'I'm *really* not enjoying this' look. I smiled at her sympathetically and squeezed her hand, glad that I was coping well. There's nothing to this navy lark, I thought...but Neptune disagreed.

Imagining I could play the sexy siren one minute and the seasoned sailor the next, vanity sent me below to gloss up my lips in my beach bag's mirror. THIS WAS A BIG MISTAKE. HUGE. As I raised my head from my rummaging, a surge of nausea the size of a tsunami swept over me and I just about managed not to upchuck right there and then. I staggered back up on deck and lowered myself down gingerly, resting my head against one of the canvas cushions. Mrs Captain offered me some cashew nuts and a glass of red wine, but I turned a whiter shade of pale, smiled weakly at her and shook my head. This was another mistake: the merest movement made the world tilt on its axis. Taking deep breaths, I concentrated on the horizon, but the nausea rose and fell like a wave machine, and I realised with the horror of inevitability that I was definitely going to throw. I fought it until I could fight it no longer, then made a clumsy dash for the rail, bashing my knee in the process, before chucking my entire guts up all over the side of the gleaming, white yacht.

Mrs Captain was incredibly kind to me. She mopped my brow, held back my hair and whispered words of comfort as she helped me back to my seat to rest my spinning head against the pillow once more. She offered me water but nothing could pass my lips. Unlike a normal bout of sickness, you only feel better momentarily before the swelling sway of the sea churns your stomach once again. People were talking and socialising all around me, but I was lost in a hazy world of misery and shame, sick as a dog and twice as ugly. My hostess suggested I might be better lying face down on the deck, so I crawled miserably on all fours and belly flopped into position, but this was another Big Mistake. Within seconds, I was retching and heaving once again, spewing bile all over my bikini as my body wracked and writhed with the ghastly degradation of it all. The Captain turned the water pipe on, pointed the jet straight at me and hosed me down like a dead haddock.

'We'll have to rename you Elizabeth Hurl-ey!' he boomed hysterically. If I'd had any guts left, I'd have throttled him with them.

Looking at, thinking of, or attempting to consort with Orlando were now totally *hors de question*. God only knew what I looked like...and the nightmare journey lasted another two hours. I sat huddled in stultified silence, my head between my legs, unable to move for fear of puking again. I dry heaved and gagged occasionally and spat up into a bucket. Oh the glamour of life on the ocean wave!

Eventually they trimmed the sails and we straightened up and cruised serenely into English Harbour and within seconds I felt perfectly well again. I went below for a shower, and revamped myself the best I could. Orlando was cooking penne all'arrabiata in the galley and in normal circumstances I'd have offered to help. Instead I took a deep breath and rose back up on deck, posing in Ta-Da! style for the others who gave me a round of applause.

'You look better!' praised Mrs Captain.

'I was fine all along!' I replied, hiding in humour. 'I just thought you guys needed a bit of entertainment!'

I wolfed down a bowl of pasta (oh! bless those carbs) and in an act of desperate sycophancy, complimented Orlando on his excellent cooking. When we left the yacht to go ashore, he was fiddling with the pump and barely looked up, so we parted again without a proper goodbye.

♀

That night E.T. had invited Lydia and me out for dinner as she'd decided to give him the benefit of the doubt. (Frogs do occasionally turn into princes but not in the real world.) Instead of being relaxed and happy, though, she looked troubled and anxious as he confidently banged on about all the wonderful things they were going to do together. Because we knew in our hearts that, for him, the end was nigh and we didn't want to take advantage, Lydia and I paid the not inconsiderable bill.

We went on to the Rasta Bar and I kept my eye on the entrance in case Someone Special ventured in. A motley crew stood around drinking, amongst them a tall, slim, handsome, steel-haired man who dispelled my theory that older men were *all* heading downhill faster than runaway wheelchairs. As E.T. and Lydia stood talking, Mr Suave caught my eye and twitched me a tiny smile. I twitched him one back. Here was a man who hadn't seen me heaving up into a bucket and that was a good thing. He had some friends drifting around but they took off and soon he was left standing on his own opposite me.

'Have you been abandoned?' I ventured boldly and he came a couple of steps closer.

We got into easy conversation about sailing and Antigua. His name was Brendan and he was from Maine. He'd left his job as a lawyer to skipper a yacht around the world for a year. He was absolutely charming and we were soon chatting away like old friends. I felt secure again, alluring, wanted. The fresh attention from a new man was healing, but my heart gave a painful lurch every time I thought of my sweet-faced Orlando and I kept an eager eye on the door.

The four of us went on to Abracadabra's, the best dance club on the island. Lydia smiled at me approvingly as Brendan held my arm to guide me along the cobbled street. We walked across the gardens and up the steps, then navigated the crowded dance floor to the bar. Brendan bought a round of drinks and we stood jiggling up and down to the hypnotic rhythms of *soca*. It was a beautiful evening spent under the stars and when we parted he kissed me affectionately on both cheeks. He said he'd look out for me the following night.

'*He* was gorgeous' said Lydia as we drove back to E.T.'s. 'That's the sort of man you should be with!'

'I know,' I said wistfully. 'He *was* lovely...' But my mind was elsewhere.

We spent the night at E.T.'s sumptuous villa. I had my own luxurious suite with a king-size bed and bathroom all to myself. What a fucking waste, I thought, as I turned off the bedside light.

The next day was New Year's Eve and the last of our week-long holiday. It must have been ordained somewhere in the annals of holiday romances that you are inevitably destined to meet somebody on your last night. This adds a terrifying speed to the proceedings which has you hurtling through it all and out the other side sooner than you can say 'What did you say your name was?' Time and geography are against you, and if you don't cram every aspect of a full-blown relationship into the space of about four hours you're going to spend the rest of your life wondering whether he may or may not have been The One.

Lydia and I got dressed in our finest and took a cab to the hub of the celebrations: English Harbour. We'd declined an invitation to eat with the yachties at $200 a head, preferring to share a steak and salad from a street barbecue. (There is definitely something in the air in Antigua that turns you stupid, crazy or both. We'd also turned down an invitation to Chris Wright's annual New Year's Eve bash because it started at 7 p.m. and we didn't want to go out so early. We later heard Eric Clapton and a host of other celebrities had been there...Doh!)

After our alfresco dinner, we had time to kill before midnight so we wandered into the Galley Bar on the waterfront. It wasn't too crowded and Lydia found a table while I went to get the drinks. I returned to where she was and checked out the chaps at the nearby tables. Directly in front of us was a group of about ten youngsters, one guy sitting slightly apart from the rest. He looked a bit like Rob Lowe and as I noticed him, he noticed me and lingered a look in my direction. You're on, I thought.

'I've pulled!' I said to Lydia, taking a long draw on my drink.

'Oh give it a rest!' she answered. 'Haven't you got into enough trouble already?'

'Insurance!' I defended. 'What if neither Brendan nor Orlando turn up tonight? Or, worse still, what if Orlando turns up draped all over some nubile blonde? I'm buggered if I'm going to spend New Year's Eve on my own!' She turned to look at the object of my attentions.

'He looks about twelve,' she commented flatly.

'Precisely!' I replied defiantly. 'He's my toyboy *du jour* – just in case.'

It only takes one drink to get me going. Trouble is I can never remember if it's the third or the fourth.

Rob Lowe and I continued our optical flirtation until Lydia got bored. E.T. as her Life Saver had been long-since dismissed and she was upset and disappointed it hadn't panned out as planned. He had houseguests over New Year so wasn't coming out until later, so she suggested we walk up the hill to Nelson's Dockyard to listen to the steel band. Rob Lowe wasn't looking in my direction as we left and I hoped he'd be sorry for that. The whole harbour area was buzzing by this time and the chance of meeting up with him again was poor to zero. Oh well, I thought as we pushed past the horde. The night is still young...

Lydia and I samba-ed to the band for a while then I dragged her back to the Galley Bar to see if Rob Lowe was still around. He wasn't but as we spilled out onto the street, he suddenly appeared about twenty yards ahead of us dancing rather drunkenly up the hill. He's a lager lout, I thought, but it didn't alter the fact that he was cute. He spotted me again and his face lit up and he started jigging towards us: three steps forward, two steps back until he was dancing at my side. I began to dance with him.

He introduced himself. His name was Johnny and he came from Seattle, which surprised me. I'd had him down as a Sarf London lad. Everyone was surging towards the main harbour as midnight struck and the fireworks started to go off. I gave Lydia a big hug and kiss and wished her Happy New Year. We stood staring up at the red, green and silver fountains exploding all around us, each of us lost in our own thoughts. In the crush, Johnny had moved behind me. He had his arms around my waist. I closed my eyes and pretended it was Orlando.

We stood ooh-ing and aah-ing at the bangs and flashes, then Johnny turned me round to face him and we began to kiss. It was 2006, the year of my 60th birthday and I was being snogged by (I later found out) a 26-year-old! Right on! Like I said, there's something in the air in Antigua...

I felt disloyal to Orlando, but Johnny was here and Orlando wasn't, and if you can't be with the one you love, you gotta love the one you're with.

For the rest of the night, Johnny never left my side. And I didn't want him to – not until about 1 a.m., when, plastered up against a tree in the dimly light gardens of Abra's with my face being snogged off, Orlando and the Canadian walked by. Shit! I moaned. F-u-u-u-c-k! I sobbed. Bugger damn and blast! I cried silently to myself. I couldn't just dump Johnny and rush to Orlando, plus all of my make-up was smudged and I must've looked like the Wreck of the Hesperus. Again.

Orlando looked absolutely gorgeous: it was the first time I'd seen him clean-shaven and properly dressed. His long, curly hair was slicked back in a ponytail and he was wearing black linen trousers and a white shirt. I buried my face in Johnny's shoulder so Orlando wouldn't see me but I peeped out at him and my heart melted and liquefied in my chest. I don't know if he saw me. I think the Canadian did. But there was nothing I could do. Crime and punishment. That was my lot.

I spent the rest of the night like Linda Blair in *The Exorcist*, swivelling my head around 360° but I never spotted him again. As dawn broke over the harbour and we hailed a cab for home, Johnny took my email address and mobile number and kissed me a long goodbye. I'd had a great time with him...but it was the wrong time and the wrong place. And though his face was lovely...it was also the wrong face... I'll spend the rest of my life wondering what would have happened if I'd been unaccompanied that night...which is a futile exercise as well I know.

♀

The self-inflicted effects of that hedonistic week in Antigua took me temporarily out of my comfort zone and into a bit of a mental maelstrom. I told everyone it was 'the best holiday I'd ever had' – it was certainly the most flattering: wall-to-wall men and most of them interested. For seven days and seven nights, Lydia and I had felt full-on fabulous, and it's hard to come down from a high like that. It made me believe Aunt Edna had been right when she'd said: 'Wendy walks into a room and all the men get an erection!'

But on returning to the freezing greyness of London in January, with everyone down in the dumps after Christmas and New Year had passed, no one even raised an eyebrow at me, never mind anything else. In Antigua, I'd been a blooming flower. In London, I was blooming invisible.

For the first few days after the holiday, my soul was in torment, obsessively replaying Orlando like a cracked record. My heart had forgotten the wisdom it had learned from past experience. Now it was stuttering, fluttering – controlling me rather than me controlling it. And I simply could not get him out of my head. I wonder if men, when they misuse a woman for their own enjoyment, suffer so badly afterwards. I hope so.

My obsession was borne of guilt mingled with regret, but my interpretation may not have been his. He'd got a shag out of it and perhaps he was satisfied with that. For my own personal closure, I would have liked to have been able to apologise. But because I had no way to contact him, I considered him lost to me forever...

And then I had an inspiration. He was arriving in London the very next morning! I knew the flight number – it was the one I'd booked for him that first evening on the internet! I'd go to the airport to meet him! I'd write him a letter and ask someone to hand it to him! I didn't really need to see him again, but I did need to absolve myself and let him know my feelings. I ran my brilliant plan past four girlfriends. None of them thought it a good idea.

I've heard it said that potential suicides feel better once they've made a firm decision. It gives them a purpose, a strategy, even something to look forward to. And so I sat down at my trusty laptop, and after much deliberation, I penned the following:

Dear 'Orlando'

This is a very challenging letter to write but because of the weird way I'm feeling, it's one I think I owe to myself and, more importantly, to you.

I want to apologise for my appalling behaviour in Antigua. God knows what you must have thought of me... I behaved like a slut which was both out of character and out of control, and I have been ashamed and mortified ever since.

I was so enjoying the good connection we'd made and I never intended it to go so far so fast – blame it on the music, the moonlight, the marijuana, too many rum punches, not enough time to consider my actions – it all just got a little bit crazy.

You are a sweet, sensitive, spiritual person and I wish we could have just talked that night, instead of me dragging you into bed. It would have been lovely just to hold you and sleep with you in an innocent way.

I never meant to abuse the situation as it spoilt the whole dynamic between us which I deeply regret.

Have a great stay in London and if you ever feel like trying out those chocolate-covered Pringles sometime, I promise to behave myself!

I decided not to remind him of the fact that he may have seen me in the arms of another on New Year's Eve. There wasn't much I could do about that...

I printed the letter out neatly and left it in an envelope by the front door. I set my alarm for 7.15 a.m. with the idea of getting to Gatwick by 9.15 a.m. The flight was due in at 9.20 a.m. I thrashed around all night until 6.35 a.m. when a moment of piercing lucidity cleared the fug from my brain and showed me what a complete idiot I was being. As my girlfriends surmised, I had totally lost the plot. I switched the alarm off and finally fell asleep.

I never expected to hear from Orlando again and I didn't. I would have liked him to know how sorry I was and I hope the experience didn't damage him or give him a bad impression about women in general, and older ones in particular. Of all my mixed-up motives, I never intended that.

So Fate threw me a curve ball and I missed the catch. Like all the other stuff of life, you just have to crack on and get over it.

BACK IN BUSINESS

Never one to let an emotional hiccup or unsatisfactory shag stop me in my pursuit of hedonism, I picked myself up, brushed myself off and by the time my 60th birthday came around in February, I was ready to start all over again. Oliver (he of the broken marriage which distracted me from Tom) made me a fabulous party at Annabel's and on the day I became an OAP, I felt positively vibrantly optimistic about the future. Three kir royales in quick succession sustained the mood, together with the fact that I had recently been introduced to an eminently suitable, though considerably older, chap. In a moment of rational madness, I got to thinking that m-a-y-b-e... just m-a-y-b-e it was time, if not actually to 'settle down', at least to settle. I mean, how bad could it be? It would be like life insurance. Make my mother happy. Stop her muttering 'God forbid you should be lonely in your old age...' like there were guarantees.

Lord Saggy Chops of Crinkly Bottom ticked a lot of my boxes but try as I might, I simply could not bring myself to get physical. I dragged the flirtation out over six dates where I got treated to opera, ballet, concerts, plays and *dîners à deux* accompanied by the finest wines and fluent conversation. This I could cope with. I enjoyed the chauffeur-driven limos and his ministering to my every need, and I stiffly tolerated the hand-holding in dark theatres, though it was like being stroked by a piece of old leather. I'd pray for the aria or solo to finish so I could extricate my mitt sharpish and clap for as long as possible before tucking my hands firmly underneath my coat to avoid him re-grabbing them. His repeated suggestions of erotic holidays in exotic locations made me shudder with dread as I imagined the unavoidable moment when he'd emerge from the bathroom, remove his navy silk polka-dot dressing-gown and reveal... whaaahh! Don't even go there... Despite his suave *savoir faire* and worldly erudition, I could not get past the fact that he looked like a Sharpei who needed ironing. And so, riddled with guilt at having availed myself of his generosity for way too long, I made my 'Sorry but...' speech and he exited my life with an angry frown and his foot hard down on the accelerator of his Bentley Arnage Grand Touring Saloon. (Retching into someone's gob while they're trying to kiss you gives off a fairly strong message, methinks!)

Bugger, I thought, as I climbed the stairs to my top floor flat. Why can't I just close my eyes and think of...a ranch hand, a rock band, Russell Brand? And I knew then that I would never settle, that I would rather hear violins for only five seconds than his snoring for the rest of my life; that I would rather eat one mouthful of tutti frutti than a whole vatful of vanilla; that I would rather live in my third floor walk-up with my Wabbit than in a castle with a frog who, no matter how many times I kissed him, would never, ever turn into a handsome Prince.

And so Sir Victor Vintage went the way of all my dear old antiques – off to find a woman who would.

The next few months passed peacefully enough. Socially, feast had turned to famine but I saw my friends, did my work, and faddled around on the internet emailing sad losers whilst pretending not to be one myself. Then one day, out of the blue, I received a sort of fan letter from a young man who'd read a magazine article I'd written lauding the merits of the older woman. He'd enjoyed the piece so much he'd contacted the editors to ask for my email address and gradually, organically, a correspondence between us ensued.

At first, we'd write to each other once or twice a week. I looked forward to his emails as they were funny and chatty, and he soon became like a pen friend to me. We exchanged photos and he looked OK and I found myself telling him stuff I wouldn't necessarily have told other people. I felt sort of safe with him in the anonymously open way one adopts when not having to make eye-contact. He had an interesting slant on how to deal with problems, and his job in I.T. enabled him to help me out every time my computer crashed.

Eventually he suggested we get together, so I cleared some space in my diary the following Sunday and he got the train down from Scotland. I went to meet him at the station, wondering momentarily as I stood on the draughty platform what I was doing yet again waiting for a complete stranger who was young enough to be my son. When Conor bounded along to greet me, I was pleasantly surprised. He was better-looking than his photo until he opened his mouth, when he revealed that not only was he missing a front tooth, but he sounded like he was talking

Norwegian. He was in fact Glaswegian with an accent so thick you could have tarmacked the road with it.

We set off on a tour of the city and I struggled to pick up one word in ten and fill in the gaps. He may have asked me: 'How long have you lived in London?' and I may have answered 'A quarter to six' – I really don't know. There was a definite language barrier. At the end of the date he tried to kiss me but what with the worry of minding the gap and the strain of following his garble all day long I was worn out and had gone off the whole idea. And so another one bit the dust... Anticipation had turned to disenchantment as I reminded myself to have no expectations and get no disappointments. Hard to live like that, though...

A few weeks later, after a fairly low period dating no one but Baron Wasteland, a friend of mine invited me to hear her son play his first gig in a local pub. It was a Sunday night and he wasn't due on until 10.30 p.m. I'd spent the evening ironing in front of the telly and when I'd finished, it would have been the normal thing to pack up and go to bed. Some higher power was driving me that night however, as I folded away the ironing board, pulled on my tightest jeans, put on some extra slap and shot down Maida Vale to *The Good Ship* in Kilburn High Road.

Jimmy was already on when I walked in but I spotted my friend with her group of wannabes and tiptoed through the tables to join her. I squeezed her hand to let her know I was there and did a quick recce of the assembled fan base. Amongst the entourage was a delicious young dude with a thick, curly pony tail who was looking daggers at three noisy girls giggling at the bar. They were dissing the singer and had he not been hemmed in at his seat, I have no doubt Pony Tail would have gone over and given them what for. I eye-candied him for a while until I caught his attention, then I cocked my head towards the disturbance and pulled a face. He nodded in agreement and we held the look a little bit longer than was necessary. My heart fluttered along with my eyelashes. When the set was over, he got up to go to the bar, and almost as an afterthought, turned around and offered me a drink.

'Why don't I buy you one?' I suggested, taking the lead as usual.

'*I'm* offering to buy *you* a drink,' he replied assertively which I liked, so I smiled sweetly and said:

'Vodka & tonic please,' relinquishing control for once.

By the time he returned with the drinks, another young stud had moved in. It was Jimmy's flatmate who was also on the right side of gorgeous and I noticed Pony Tail's face drop as he hovered near the table holding our glasses. I beckoned for him to return to my side and looking somewhat relieved, he sat down close to me allowing his leg to loll against mine. I didn't move away. We chatted about the music and how we'd both nearly not come, and I asked him what he did for a living. Since he was wearing a tracksuit and sporting a thick Essex accent I was not surprised to learn, when he gave me his card, that he was neither a lawyer nor an accountant but a plasterer. Well you can get me plastered any time, honey! Around midnight, with everyone having drifted off home and the owners trying to close the joint, we peeled ourselves away from each other and he asked if he could call me sometime. For some reason best known to the Untruth Fairy, I told him I was busy for the next three weeks (Duh!) but I wrote my mobile on the back of his card and gave it back to him. (Double Duh! Now I didn't have his number!) He walked me to my car and kissed me gently three times on the mouth. On the fourth, he parted his lips a little and snaked his tongue lightly against mine. I got a lustful blood rush but pressed my palms flat against his firm pecs, gave him a gentle push and said: 'Go!' Then I drove home humming a love song with a stupid grin on my face.

The following day by a roundabout, convoluted and circuitous route, I obtained his number on the pretext of having a friend who needed a new kitchen. Well 'e's a builder, in 'e? I texted him and he texted me back and this continued throughout the week until the following Sunday, when he arrived to pick me up for our first date. Kitchen Schmitchen! A girl's gotta do what a girl's gotta do. He hugged me hallo and immediately confessed to being very nervous.

'Why?' I asked innocently as if I didn't know.

'I've never dated an older woman before,' he replied with a beguiling honesty. 'I'm not sure what we'll find to talk about.'

A bubble appeared above my head with the motif: who wants to talk?

'Don't worry!' I said pouring him a large drink and putting him at his ease. 'I'm a little nervous myself. But we're just two people. And two people can always find something to talk about.'

And we smiled endearingly at each other and clinked glasses.

We set off in his nice, clean car which turned out to belong to his father. I'm sixty years old and I'm dating a man who lives with his parents! But he was so cool to be with, so funny, down-to-earth and open, so charismatic and attentive. And I felt completely myself with him. When he took my hand as we walked from the car to the restaurant I came over all girly. That public demonstration of affection meant a lot to me and pleased me no end. All the youthful vigour I had so missed sprang out of him and into me and though he treated me like a lady, he made me feel like a teenager.

After dinner, we drove to the cinema where he insisted on paying despite my offer to buy the tickets since he'd bought the meal.

'I'm taking you out!' he stated and stood behind me in the queue with his arms wrapped around me nuzzling my neck. I felt very young and very happy. I did, however, have an economic dilemma on his behalf at the box office when I wondered fleetingly whether I should mention that I qualified for the senior discount! I decided for once, to keep my lip zipped.

In true first-date style, we sat in the back row mouth-feeding each other chocolate raisins thereby missing half the film. Who cared? And on returning home, unlike men my own age who ought to know better, he double-parked as if the date was over.

'Wouldn't you like to come up?' I asked, barely concealing a bleat of desperation in my voice. Don't Go Yet, I Haven't Finished With You!

'I'd love to,' he answered. 'I just didn't want to appear presumptuous, that's all.'

And again I am blown away by this delightful geezer with his arrested education and respectful manners.

I light the fire and the candles, put on some music, pour the drinks and for the next two hours, my baby and I kiss, cuddle and have simulated sex on my sofa. Very, very slowly, as the vodka and passion take hold, the layers are peeled away until I am burning with the desire to feel this fit, young turk's bare skin next to mine. I unbutton his shirt, lift off my top and remove my bra, and with a shuddering sigh I rest myself against him. Once my naked breasts are touching his naked chest, I am lost...and despite my best intentions, I lead him (not unwillingly I suppose) into my fantasy where we make sweet, sensual love until the dawn.

(I'm sorry. I've got friends my age who've already died. I simply had to seize the moment.)

The date ends at 6.45 a.m. when he leaves me splashed across my wrecked bed with a glazed expression of blissful ecstasy on my face.

Mercifully, allowing him his wicked way (or me mine) on the first date did not affect the continuance of our relationship. As far as older women were concerned, this manchild was converted. Four fun-filled weeks later we are still together with plans into the next few months. He wants to learn. I love to teach. He likes to talk. I shut up and listen. He wants a girlfriend. I need this man.

Of course, there is a bittersweet sorrow to all of this. On saying goodbye after our second date, a tiny crack fractures my heart and I know from past experience that I am becoming attached.

Stop that at once! I tell myself as I sway dreamily to some sloshy ballad. Tired and emotional, I text him that if I was halfway sensible, I would end it now before I get hurt. He replies mildly panicked that I have dumped him, and says he also has feelings for me. He says he knows we cannot be together forever which deeply saddens him. (Of course, my forever is much shorter than his...) My best friend reminds me that I may tire of him before he tires of me so I pull myself together and decide to enjoy it for what it is. He is a wonderful, caring, savvy, perceptive young man who has not had it easy. He excites all my instincts but he loves children and must, at some point, have his own. I already love him a little but one day I shall have to love him enough to let him go. But for now, I am happier than I have been for a long time. I've met his cousins and his father on our date to the Arsenal; he's met my younger daughter (who asked me reproachfully if he was old enough to vote!)

He is just twenty-eight. I'm nearly sixty-one. If anyone has any objection to this, will they speak now or forever hold their peace. I know which piece I'll be holding.

Rock on!

AFTERGLOW

When a random turn or two brought me more than once to the edge, I did not topple into the tangled mysteries below. But on that glassy threshold, the great strengths of my life pressed themselves into being - my illusive tools for survival, gifts from some primeval ancestor, passed in secret along the chain of my forebears.

In the end, mine is a navigator's sense of place and the strength again to hoist the sails, the will again to catch the winds, and even when the land and all I ever loved are lost to me, and the stars are shrouded, and I am sore with losses and afraid – even then, the miracles all around will leap to celebrate themselves, and I will celebrate them too.

And even then, I'll trust that a new shore will rise to meet me and there, in that new place, I will find new things to care about.

Mia Farrow – *What Falls Away*

That passage is my inspiration and I have often drawn on it to help me through some wobbly times – wobblies, it has to be said, of my own making. Toyboys are clearly not a recipe for peace and tranquillity and the emotional ride from my nefarious escapades has often played havoc with my personal wellbeing and the supposed enjoyment of my advancing years. But I say Pah! to all that. There is an unjust dichotomy about growing old: the cruel twist is that everything ages except your feelings.

You've probably noticed a recurring theme in all these stories. Boy meets girl, boy shags girl, boy leaves girl. Why does she do it, I hear you ask? I do it because I can, because of how it makes me feel. I love the reflection of being with a younger man – they mirror the me I'd like to be. It's youth by association. Youth by injection. Better than botox any day.

Revisiting my sex life has meant hours of deep introspection which has peppered my brain with a mélange of mixed emotions. I'm amazed that I got away with so much: no hideous diseases, no brutal rapes, no ugly encounters and no permanent brain damage. I bent, oh yes I bent...but I never broke.

So what have I learned from my relentless pursuit of hedonism?

I've learned that you can never have too much sex.

I've learned that it's better to suffer a Brazilian than to shave.

I've learned that, even with brand new batteries, I can only climax five times.

I've learned that when it comes to men, I'll never learn.

I'm sure I've driven my girlfriends mad with my endless crowing about my conquests, often when their social cupboards have been sadly bare. But even if they found my behaviour questionable (and they did) they were always there to pick up the pieces and listen to my wailing when it all went wrong.

I advocate that women need to live more like men – especially when they haven't got one. Of course we love being wooed and that will never change, but in a wham-bam context, sometimes it's better to be the whammer than the whammee.

With the passage of time and the inevitable erosion of

my looks, despite my devout worship at the great shrine of Boots the Chemist, I accept the fact that the best is *not* yet to come. This is simply another challenge, and like all challenges it has to be faced, defied and overcome. I've tried not to let real life get in the way of my dreams – *au contraire*, my dreams have often got in the way of real life.

I am resolutely unconvinced that I need a proper relationship. For as we all know, where there is love, pain is never far behind... If, however, the right one comes along, I shall welcome him with open arms. If he does not, I shall smile wistfully, open the catch on my memory bank and be thankful.

Each of my adventures has been life-enhancing and I wouldn't have missed them for the world. Topographically speaking, I prefer being the fairground than the heath.

To all the boys I've known before, I'd like to say one last thing:

'Gentlemen! Please continue to be upstanding' – and in the words of comic genius Eric Idle:

'Fuck you very much!'

ACKNOWLEDGEMENTS

Without the unconditional support and persistent doubting of my beloved homies, this book would never have been finished. Mostly they asked: 'Are you mad? Why tell the world your sordid little secrets? Think of your children, your mother...' but I ploughed on relentlessly.

My thanks to my big sister Marilyn: indulgent in every way. My thanks to Adrianne: a great listener, adviser and Life Coach Extraordinaire. To Bernice: my daily sounding-board and guideline to the straight and narrow. To Karen: my confrontational Scrabble partner. To Frances: 'It's only been a day, dear' and to Maggi: the yin to my yang, much-respected Jungian Therapist and a stabilising influence in my crazy world...and to all the other girlfriends who misguidedly call me a role model and an inspiration. I only ever try to be my best self.

Thanks also to my stable of suitables for your delightful company. If any of these revelations have shocked and appalled you, I'm afraid t
hat's your problem. I could say I made them all up...and maybe I did...or maybe even the lies I tell aren't true...

And last but not least, a heartfelt thanks to my agent, Adrian Weston at Raft PR & Representation, who believed in my story sufficiently to tout it around the world. And thanks also to the wonderful team at Old Street Publishing, who've made me feel that something I tiddled with of an evening in my back bedroom is a work of worth. Thank you all!

TESTIMONIALS

From the age of thirteen, Wendy used her pussy power to seduce the Girls' Hockey Team. Then she discovered men and I lost her. Bitch...we could have had a future...

Margery Dunston – Notting Hill Convent School for Girls

Wendy's style, *savoir faire* and acid one-liners drew men to her like drunks to a brewery. I was just one of many, hoping for a kiss...a touch...something...anything! Maybe if I'd bought that nose-hair trimmer things could've been different... Excuse me...I have to go and lie down.

Cyril – social reject, aged 73

Age cannot wither her nor custom stale her infinite variety.

Will Shakespeare

When Wendy walks into a room, all the men get an erection.

Aunt Edna, aged 87

She's a tramp but I love her, breaks a new heart every day.

Walt Disney

Sucks like a Dyson.

Kris, 22

Great tits!

Dr Peregrine Carleton-Browne – Consultant Gynaecologist